Born 9 Nov 1841
Lewis Nathan, son of George
and Isabella Benjamin
G H Benjamin

Born 6 July 1844
Ellis Ralph, son of George and
Isabella Benjamin
G H Benjamin

Born 9 Decr 1845
Harry Aaron, son of George and
Isabella Benjamin
G H Benjamin
Born 21 Decr 1847
Frederick Philip son of George
and Isabella Benjamin

Beatstock
5/15

BURN THIS GOSSIP

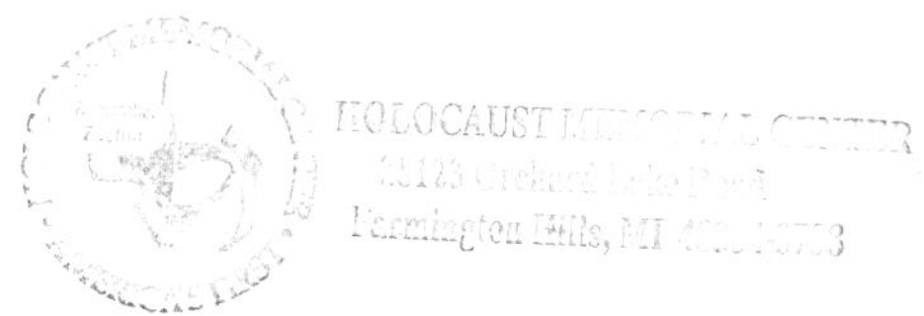

The True Story of
George Benjamin of Belleville
Canada's First Jewish
Member of Parliament
1857-1863

Sheldon and Judith Godfrey

THE DUKE & GEORGE PRESS

Printed in Canada

Produced by WordsWorth Communications of Toronto, Canada, using Microsoft® Word and PageMaker® on the Apple® Macintosh™ computer. Camera-ready pages produced on the LaserMAX 1000™.

Canadian Cataloguing in Publication Data

Godfrey, Sheldon, 1938-
   Burn this gossip : the true story of George
Benjamin of Belleville, Canada's first Jewish Member
of Parliament 1857-1863

Includes index.
ISBN 0-9695102-0-9

1. Benjamin, George, 1799-1864. 2. Canada.
Parliament. House of Commons – Biography.
3. Legislators – Canada – Biography. 4. Politicians –
Canada – Biography. 5. Orangemen – Canada –
Biography. 6. Jews – Canada – Biography. I. Godfrey,
Judith, 1940-   . II. Title.

FC471.B4G6 1991   328.71'092   091-093689-7
F1032.B4G6 1991

Published with the assistance of the Ontario Heritage Foundation, Ontario Ministry of Culture and Communications.

The Duke & George Press
49 Front Street East
Toronto, Ontario
M5E 1B3

"So get ready like a good fellow, I won't listen to your retiring into private life, until you have returned to your constituents and got their approbation. Do not be a horse for *one heat* only ... .

After by the aid of yourself & others, we are firmly in the Saddle for 4 years I am quite ready to see that you are provided for in a manner suitable to your standing & gratifying to your friends — I mentioned several contingencies to you — all of which will be available at the right time ... .

However enough of this. Burn this gossip."

John A. Macdonald to George Benjamin
4 November 1857

CONTENTS

FOREWORD

This book provides an insight into the story of George Benjamin, who was the first Jewish member of a Canadian parliament and who became, in 1862, the first Jew to be asked to sit as a minister in a Canadian cabinet. He refused the position because his political loyalty was to the opposition party of the day, which was led by John A. Macdonald. This offer, made to Benjamin, by John Sandfield Macdonald, came 107 years before I was honoured to become in 1969 Canada's first federal cabinet minister of the Jewish faith.

The significance of Benjamin's biography is twofold. At one level it shows where the Province of Canada (since 1867 the provinces of Ontario and Quebec) stood on the matter of civil and political rights. The authors of this book will be documenting the development of these rights in Canada and comparing its record with those of the United States and England in a subsequent work. At another level, Benjamin's biography explores the tension between being a Jew in preconfederation Canada and aspiring to the exercise of full and equal civil and political rights.

George Benjamin was astute and apparently well educated, and had drawn inspiration from a family which came to be noted on three continents for uncommon achievements in the the fields of journalism and politics. By the end of his career, all but the highest government offices had come within his reach. As this book shows, while Benjamin had built bridges and overcome obstacles, religious and ethnic factors were still of importance to the personalities of the day.

George Benjamin made major strides. His pioneering efforts helped confirm the rights and freedoms of future generations of Canadians of different religious and cultural origins.

The Honourable Herb Gray, PC, MP
Ottawa
12 February 1991

PREFACE

It started off innocently enough. Judy and I were in the Kingston Public Library on a hot summer's day at the beginning of August 1986. We had been conducting our own spare-time research project to try to uncover information about Jewish settlement in Canada in the period of the first English settlements. Our interest had been sparked by something someone had said about there not being any Jews before 1840 in what is now Ontario. We had checked recently published works and found that no one had yet gone into the primary sources on the subject in any depth. Based on research we had done previously and on our own sense of how the country had been settled, we were positive that there was significant settlement by Jews along with other English-speaking settlers all across the country right from the beginning.

And we were finding evidence. Lots of it. Our vacations had become an odyssey that led us through public archives — the National Archives in Ottawa, the provincial archives in Ontario, Quebec, the Maritimes, and Newfoundland — and that had led us to smaller collections of documents as well. In the latter category, we had had trips all over the eastern half of North America to the archives of universities, synagogues, state and local historical societies, county land registry offices, surrogate or probate courts, and public libraries.

We were beginning to piece together stories of a number of individuals who were Jewish but who had little or no formal connection with any Jewish community and whose existence had not previously been discovered. Many of these individuals were happy to forget their roots and blend into the religion of the vast majority of the population. They were none the less perceived as Jewish by those who knew them, and had a significant impact on the development of concepts of equal rights for minorities in the country.

We had developed a fairly long list of names of individuals that we had confirmed were Jewish by conviction or ancestry. One of our standard searches was to check off the names in the catalogue of each of the institutions we visited to see if we could find additional information.

That brought us to Kingston. Many of the public libraries in Ontario have recently completed projects of indexing newspapers or genealogical materials in their collections. The Kingston Public Library's contribution to this effort is an enormous card index of virtually all names and events referred to in local newspapers from about 1800 to 1850. We were certain we would find lots of new information.

When we arrived in the library I at once started my searches in the index. I am fairly structured in my approach. I take lists and check them off. I go through notes I have made previously and try to follow up leads.

Judy has a more lateral approach to research. She is always looking sideways, if that is the right word, to see what can be discovered by looking at the edges of the structured approach. For example, whenever we come to a new archives, we invariably have an introductory talk with an archivist who asks us what we are looking for. This is a natural enough question for a helpful person in charge of a collection of documents. It leads researchers with specific questions to specific answers if the material is in the collection. Judy never tells the archivist exactly what we are looking for even though I always try. Instead, she always asks the archivist what is in the institution's collection, the theory being that we do not know what we can find until we know what they have got. In any event, after our initial interview with an archivist, I always go to the catalogues and look up specific things, and Judy always sits with her pad and pencil and reviews all the names in all the catalogues to try to figure out the collection by herself.

While I was looking up names and leads in the Kingston newspaper index, Judy was looking up the catalogue. When she came to the index card for "Jew," she came across some interesting entries from the *British Whig*. One, dated 3 November 1835, stated that "G. Benjamin, the editor of *The Belleville Intelligencer*, objects to being called a Jew in a derogatory sense." Another, from 26 April 1837, reported that "George Benjamin the editor was hanged in effigy. Copy of a poem entitled 'The execution of the Belleville Jew'." Again, on 11 May 1838, an article about "George Benjamin, Editor of The Belleville Intelligencer. The *British Whig* editor states that he is a Jew, and, because of his religion under British law cannot hold a captaincy in the militia unless he converts to Christianity."

We were both excited to have found a name that was not on our list. We wanted more information as fast as possible. We went to the section of the library where the *Dictionary of Canadian Biography* is kept on the off chance that there might be some small reference to George Benjamin.

He was there all right, in volume IX. It was more than just a reference. There was a whole article about him. It said where and when he was born and when he died. It said that he held office as a politician. It said that he was the grand master of the Orange lodges of British North America. But it did not say he was Jewish. And it did not give any information about his parents or relatives. That was not the way he was remembered.

Over the next few months we concentrated our research energies on finding out more about the mysterious George Benjamin. In the collections of the Hastings County Historical Society held by the Belleville Public Library, we found a number of Benjamin family papers deposited by a great grand-daughter named Georgia, who was descended from the Benjamins' daughter Georgia. Judy was particularly interested to learn that George Benjamin had changed his name from Cohen as she is also from a Cohen family. We found that he had come from Brighton, England. We learned that the Benjamins' descendants are all Christian and that they believed George had also become Christian somewhere along the way, even though he was born Jewish. There was quite a bit of additional information.

I looked up Georgia's phone number in the Belleville directory but there was nothing there. The papers in the library had referred to her daughter Kathy. I found her number in the directory. But I did not call. I did not feel comfortable.

Following up the Cohens of Brighton seemed like a hopeless task. By now, we had a good understanding of how historical records are kept in

North America. We also had a reasonable familiarity with published works, and how to access them. England was another story. It was not just the distance and the fact that questions had to be asked by letter, and that answers took months to come. English records are kept in an entirely different system, which we had never had the opportunity to use, and English published works and periodicals — particularly local histories on Jewish subjects — are not readily available in North America.

We had one tenuous lead. About a year earlier I had written to the synagogue in Plymouth, England, to try to get information about a man named Moses Jacobs, who was apparently from Plymouth and who lived in Kingston, Upper Canada, in the period before 1800. The synagogue had no knowledge of Jacobs but they did send me a well-researched pamphlet on "The Old Jewish Cemetery on Plymouth Hoe," written by Rabbi B. Susser a few years earlier.

We thought we would use the same technique for Brighton. I called up the office of the British Consulate in Toronto and asked them for the names and addresses of all the synagogues in Brighton, England. There was only one — the Brighton and Hove Hebrew Synagogue. What made me start was the name of its rabbi, a gentleman named Dr B. Susser. Did I dare to hope that Rabbi B. Susser, the local historian of Plymouth, had moved to Brighton and would help me solve a mystery? I wrote at once, telling him what I knew of the story, and asking if he could tell me more. The reply came from David Spector of Hove. He told me that Rabbi Susser had moved on two years earlier, but that he, David Spector, had made a study of the Jews of Brighton and had delivered a paper to the Jewish Historical Society of England on the subject in 1968.

Paydirt!

We had stumbled into the network! David Spector is the foremost authority on the Jews of Brighton. He sent me a copy of his scholarly essay on "The Jews of Brighton, 1770-1900," which had been published in the *Transactions of the Jewish Historical Society of England* in 1970. There was a wealth of information in the article about George Benjamin's family. David Spector also put me in touch with Theodore Marx, an amateur historian and genealogist who had made a study of the Cohen family. Anne Marx, his wife, was actually a descendant of the Cohens of

Brighton. There was more research that Theo Marx and David Spector shared with us. One thing that had seemed particularly fascinating was that the Cohen family tree did not include George Benjamin among the ten children of Emanuel Hyam Cohen and Hannah Benjamin. It was as if at some point he had been dropped from the family records, in spite of the fact that their research contained a copy of a letter from George Benjamin in Belleville to his brother Abraham Cohen in Australia. After our contact, their family trees were corrected and our research was starting to take shape.

On 29 November 1986, we had an accidental contact with another Benjamin descendant. Judy and I had been asked to present an award for architectural excellence to the Elmwood Club in Toronto on behalf of the Architectural Conservancy of Ontario. Just before the ceremony, Alec Keefer, the president of the Conservancy, asked what we had been doing recently. I mentioned, in general terms, that we had been researching early Jewish settlement in Canada. "You would probably have a lot to talk about with one of my neighbours," he said. "She is always talking about her great grandfather who was a politician. I think his name was George Benjamin."

The next day we spent two hours on the phone with Nancy. Her grandfather, Lewis Nathan Benjamin, was George Benjamin's second son. She was as interested in the story of George Benjamin as we were. (It was our lucky day for more reasons than having reached Nancy: that night we won a door prize that was to pay for our trip to England.) Within a week we had met Nancy a number of times and I had seen her amazing collection of original family letters, photographs, and even oil portraits of George Benjamin and his wife Isabella, done in the 1840s. In another week I had visited with Dorothy, Nancy's sister, and seen more letters and pictures.

Nancy had never heard of Georgia or Kathy, and she knew nothing about the Cohens of Brighton. I gave Nancy the phone number I received from the Belleville directory for Kathy. Nancy called and, after the introductions, was given Georgia's number. Nancy and Georgia talked, visited, and decided that they were so remarkably similar that neither of them could get a word in edgewise when they were together. We visited

Georgia too. She was as interested in the story as the rest of us. She had a number of family artifacts that helped explain the story of George Benjamin.

Nancy was able to go to England the following year and meet the Marxes and the Spectors. And Judy and I, after a number of other trips, were able to piece together a remarkable record that tells a story long forgotten.

◆

The notes at the end of chapters are not included merely as academic documentation, but as an enrichment of the story. In many cases they constitute asides, which would otherwise detract from the fluency of the work, but which provide interesting additional information and suggestions for further research.

Although an enormous amount of documentation has surfaced in the researching of this biography, unfortunately a number of important sources have not been located. Almost all the issues of the Belleville *Intelligencer*, between the time it was founded by George Benjamin in 1834 and the year 1856, have not survived. Thus, an exceptionally important source for detail of Benjamin's years as owner, publisher, and editor of the paper is missing. Again, references have been found suggesting that Benjamin had a number of scrapbooks, meticulously detailing events in his career. The scrapbooks are similarly not available.

As a result, in the few instances where direct evidence of material fact is no longer available, conclusions have been sketched out on the basis of the evidence available in the form of other sources and contemporary accounts. These conclusions have been used only to re-establish the setting of events, rather than the content of the events themselves. In particular, the settings described in chapters I, III, V, and XV have been reconstructed in this manner. Where circumstantial details have been used, they have been indicated in the text or chapter notes, together with references to supporting evidence.

Sheldon Godfrey
Toronto, February 1991

ACKNOWLEDGEMENTS

WE WOULD LIKE TO EXPRESS OUR APPRECIATION TO THOSE WHO HAVE SHARED their research with us or given us clues for further investigation. These include: David Spector, the acknowledged authority on the history of the Jews of Brighton; Theodore Marx, the Cohen family genealogist; Gerald E. Boyce, Belleville's unofficial resident historian; Nancy Cooper, for her assistance and encouragement; Patricia Fleming and Elizabeth Hulse, who directed us to information regarding George Benjamin and the founding of the *Intelligencer*; and Michael Peterman of Trent University, biographer of Susanna Moodie.

This book could not have been written without the assistance of the Benjamin family: Georgia, Nancy, and Dorothy, and their relatives, including Anne Marx of England and Henry Robert Cohen of Australia. There are others who made this book possible, among them David Roberts, who edited the manuscript and gave us direction and support; Paula Pike, who organized its publication; Lynda Kovacevic, Margaret Talley, and Christine Brush, who bore the brunt of much of the detail; and M. J. Samuels and Alex Camp, who gave us the benefit of their experience in photography. Still others read the manuscript at different stages or gave us helpful suggestions, including Dr Donald Akenson, Phyllis Bruce, Michael and Hilary Cole, Jane Griesdorf, Don Lake, Malcolm Lester, Phyllis Mankoff, Jack and Connie Sword, and Mary Woods. Our sons, William, Michael, and Jonathan, all helped with the research and did more legwork than any of us anticipated.

We must also acknowledge the courtesy, assistance, and support we have had in our research from the staffs of institutions and repositories of collections of documents, including Ruth Stacey Riggs of the Anglican Diocesan Centre in Kingston, Ontario; Betsy Boyce, Marion Fisher, and the Hastings County Historical Society; the Canadian Jewish Archives, Montreal, and David Rome, its director emeritus; the staff of the Hastings County Museum; Carl Bateman, clerk of Hastings County and his staff; the Belleville *Intelligencer*; the staffs of the reference departments of Belleville's Corby Public Library, the Kingston Public Library, and the Baldwin Room of the Metropolitan Toronto Reference Library; Tom Hillman, Patricia Kennedy, and Lawrence Tapper of the National Archives of Canada; Eugene Martel, John Mezzacks, Cathy Shepard, and Leon Warmski of the Archives of Ontario; the staff of the Australian Jewish Historical Society in Sydney; Beverly Davis of the Australian Jewish Historical Society in Melbourne; Marty and Estelle Kosoy of the Toronto Jewish Historical Society; and Jerry L. Cross of the North Carolina Department of Cultural Resources.

Finally, we would like to acknowledge publicly our debt to our family and friends, who allowed the subject matter of this book to intrude in one way or another into most of our conversations over the last five years.

CHAPTER I

Toronto, 1834

"Of all the places I ever saw this, the
Capital of His Majesty's Province of U.C. is the most
dirty. I do not know but a light bark canoe might sail through
the muddy streets. An Act of Incorporation is talked of and
then perhaps the lapse of a few years may make the
Town tolerable for pedestrians."

John Mann, York, 10 December 1833

THE SMALL SHIP TOUCHED THE WHARF AND WAS IMMEDIATELY MADE FAST TO its moorings. It had landed at Toronto, the provincial capital of Upper Canada, after a short voyage from Niagara across Lake Ontario.[1] The water was cold, the ice having only just left the harbour, and the crew carefully laid out the gangway to let the passengers disembark in safety. It was April 1834.[2]

A man in his mid thirties, his jacket rumpled from a long trip, stood on the deck. From the few words he spoke, he seemed well educated and English born, but it was his unusual appearance that distinguished him from the other passengers. He was short and fat, with broad shoulders, and a head and neck like a bull's. The unusual size of his head was rendered more remarkable by the quantity of coarse, curling black hair, which set off his rich, dark complexion. The features of his face were thick, the outline regular, and he might have been considered by many to be good looking, even handsome. His prominent black eyes were partially concealed by a pair of gold-rimmed spectacles, which never parted from his large aquiline nose. A perpetual grin severed his red pursed lips, displaying a set of strong white teeth.[3]

In his shadow, a girl, not more than 14, pressed beside him, followed closely by a black woman holding what appeared to be the girl's baby. They stood on the wharf in the manner of immigrants on the threshold of a new life in a new country, and watched for their baggage to be removed from the ship. In his hand, the man carried a small satchel. Inside, among his few personal belongings, was a small leather-bound book printed entirely in Hebrew.

The title page of the book indicated that it was a prayer-book for the holy day of Rosh Hashonah — the Jewish New Year — according to the Ashkenazic or German tradition, and that it had been printed in Amsterdam in the 1780s by the House of Proops. At the bottom of the

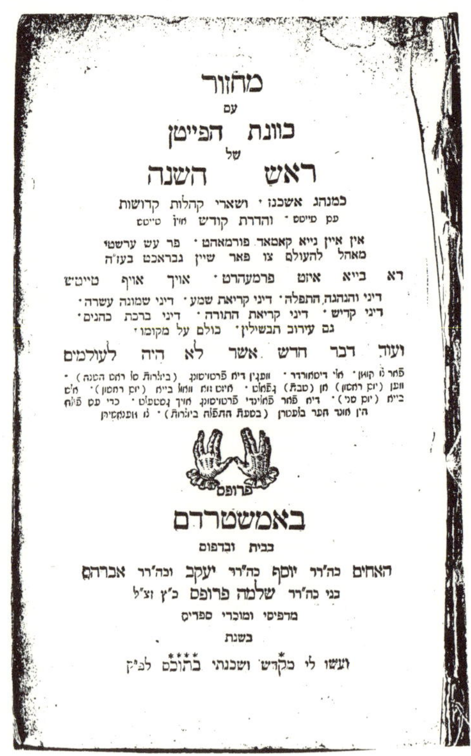

Title page of George Benjamin's Hebrew prayer-book,
published by Proops in Amsterdam in the 1780s.

title page was an imprint of a printer's mark composed of two hands, the palms facing the reader, with lace at the wrists. On each hand the second and third fingers were spread apart in the manner of the high priest of the Jews during the priestly blessing.[4] Proops' printer's mark announced that its maker was a descendant of the *cohen* or priestly class. On the end-paper at the left side of the book there were a number of entries, in pen, written in English. The first was an announcement: "Married, 5 February 1832 George Benjamin to Isabella Jacobs." Not included in the announcement was the information that Isabella Jacobs had been born in New Orleans on 8 March 1819 and was not quite 13 years of age at the date of her marriage. Her husband, born in Brighton, England, on 15 April 1799, was almost 33. The second entry followed closely after the first: "Born 21st November 1832 Emanuel Hyman Son of George and Isabella Benjamin." This entry was signed "G. Benjamin." Emanuel Hyman Benjamin had been named after his paternal grandfather, Emanuel Hyam Cohen, who died in Brighton in 1823.

Among his possessions the man carried a small seal with a wooden handle and a brass face — the kind used for making an imprint of a personal mark in sealing wax. A breastplate was engraved on the brass face, topped by an impression of the hands of the high priest of the Jews in the posture of the priestly blessing.[5] On closer examination it was apparent that the representation of the hands on the seal was identical to hands of the printer's mark in the Hebrew book even to the lace ruffles

George Benjamin's family seal.

at the wrists on both sets of hands. Solomon ben Joseph Proops, the founder of Amsterdam's House of Proops, a firm of Hebrew publishers, had used the hands as a printer's mark to indicate his priestly descent as a member of the Cohen family. The Proops of Amsterdam had begun their activity at about the time of the death of Gershom ben Solomon Kohen of Prague, the leader of the first major family of Hebrew printers, who issued his first printed prayer-book in 1512. It was Kohen of Prague, also known as Hakohen or Katz,[6] who had first adopted a printer's mark of hands in the posture of the priestly blessing — again an identical posture, even to the lace at the wrists.[7] Was there a connection between George Benjamin, the bearer of the prayer-book and seal, the Kohens of Prague, and the Proops of Amsterdam?

George Benjamin, c. 1833.

Though by no means the first Jew in Upper Canada, George Benjamin was to leave an enormous mark on his adopted country. He was the first Jewish notary public appointed by a Canadian government, the first Jew known to have been elected to municipal office in Canada, the first Jewish county registrar of deeds, and Canada's first Jewish justice of the peace. He was to become, with one possible exception, the first Jew permitted to retain a seat as a member in a Canadian parliament, before Jews had sat in the Parliament of Great Britain or the legislatures of most of the American states. Before his career ended, he would be the first Jew to be offered a position in the cabinet of the government of the Province of Canada, more than a hundred years before the next Jewish member of parliament was offered a federal cabinet position.

NOTES

[1] The setting for the Benjamins' arrival in Toronto is suggested by a memorandum written by Isabella Pauline Georgia Milburn, daughter of George and Isabella Benjamin, George Benjamin file, item no. 2385 in the Hastings County Historical Society Collection in Belleville's Corby Public Library. It says in part: "Mother's Father allowed one of his Woman Slaves to come out with Mother — to take care of Maurice 3 months old," a possible reference to Emanuel Hyman Benjamin, born 21 November 1832. There is no doubt the Benjamins would have reached Canada from the southern United States through New York: up the Hudson River, along the Erie Canal (completed 1825) to one of the ports on the south side of Lake Ontario, then across by steamboat. According to one contemporary observer, the whole trip from New York to Canada could be completed in not much more than three days as "you have water carriage every foot of the way ... . Do not come by Quebec as there have been thirteen wrecks already, 600 lives lost, and it is a very tedious passage." William Hutton, Belleville, to his wife Fanny in Ireland, 8 June 1834, cited in Gerald E. Boyce, *Hutton of Hastings* (Hastings County Council, Ontario Intelligencer Limited, Belleville, 1972), p. 33.

[2] The date of the Benjamins' arrival in Toronto is based on circumstantial evidence, but it occurred between March 1833 and April 1834. George Benjamin founded the *Intelligencer* in Belleville in August 1834. There are many documentary references to him after that date. No other documentary references relating to him

before that date have been found. The suggestion of the earlier date arises as a result of a summary of the official records of the Provincial Grand Orange Lodge of Ontario East prepared about 1940, indicating that in 1833 Benjamin was granted the original warrant for the establishment of Lodge No. 102 for meetings at Roslin in Thurlow Township, County of Hastings. (Records in possession of the current Grand Secretary, Loyal Orange Lodge, Keith McCooeye of Gloucester, Ontario.) As copies of the original warrant for Lodge No. 102 can no longer be located, it is not known if the warrant was actually given to Benjamin in 1833, or issued in 1833 and given to Benjamin, as its first official, at a later date. According to his obituary, written by his close friend and protégé Mackenzie Bowell, Benjamin had immigrated to Toronto from North Carolina and had come to Belleville in 1834 ("George Benjamin, Esq.," *Intelligencer,* 9 September 1864). Additional support for the earlier date is the account written by the Benjamins' daughter Georgia about 100 years after the event, stating that at the time of their departure for Canada the Benjamins had a child "Maurice 3 months old" (see note 1). If "Maurice" was Emanuel Hyman, their first child (who was usually referred to as "Mannie" in family correspondence), this fact would date their departure from the South at the end of February 1833, as Emanuel was born 21 November 1832. On the other hand, Benjamin's newspaper advertisement announcing his commencement of business in Toronto on 11 July 1834 is probably conclusive evidence of his arrival in Toronto in that year. *Infra,* chapter II, p. 15.

3   This description of George Benjamin has been adapted from Susanna Moodie's hostile description in "Richard Redpath a Tale," published in the *Literary Garland,* new series, volume I (Montreal, Lovell and Gibson, 1843), p. 484. There was no doubt Benjamin was the subject of the description. "The Jew Editor," she later wrote her publisher, "is a true picture drawn from life which so closely resembles the original that it will be recognized by all who ever knew him, or fell under his lash. A man detested in his day and generation." Susanna Moodie, Belleville, to Richard Bentley, London, 30 January 1854 in Carl Ballstadt *et al., Susanna Moodie: letters of a lifetime* (Toronto, University of Toronto Press, 1985), p. 147.

4   The "priestly blessing" is benediction chanted by the *cohanim* or members of the priestly class, standing in front of the congregation in the synagogue as part of festival and holy-day services, following the formula in Numbers 6:24-26. The blessing has been customarily translated: "The Lord bless you and keep you; the Lord make His face to shine upon you and be gracious unto you; the Lord lift up His countenance upon you and grant you peace."

5   A description on the seal was given by George Benjamin to a brother 30 years later: "The seal you speak of is in the hands of my eldest son. On the Shield are the [cohen's] hands. [As to the five circles] these indicate the tents, the Lamb is the pascal lamb, [the rectangle with twelve squares indicates] The breastplate to which the high Priest alone had right, and I take it if we are to trust the Name we were the lineal offspring from the First High Priest on record, Aaron. Our name was not

simply [Cohen] but [Hacohen] and then the Lion rampant." (Translations of the original Hebrew lettering or symbols appear here in brackets.) George Benjamin to Abraham Cohen, Abraham Cohen family papers in the possession of the family, Sydney, Australia.

6   The possibility exists that George Benjamin's "Hakohen" family, which had lived in Niederwerren, near Munich, was related to the "Hakohen" family of Gershom ben Solomon Kohen of Prague.

7   Raphael Posner and Israel Ta-Shema, eds., *The Hebrew Book, An historical survey* (New York-Paris, Leon Amiel Publisher, 1975), "Kohen," pp. 156-58, "Proops," p. 159, and "Printers' Marks," pp. 199-200.

CHAPTER II

From Brighton to Belleville

ॐ

> "We were the lineal offspring of the first high priest on record,
> Aaron. Our name was not simply Cohen, but Hacohen."
>
> *George Benjamin to his brother Abraham Cohen, 6 May 1864*

UNLIKE MOST PEOPLE OF HIS TIME, GEORGE BENJAMIN WAS ABLE TO TRACE HIS ancestors to the 15th century, when the Ha-Kohen family fled the Inquisition in Spain.[1] His great-grandfather, Don Menachen ben Chajim Ha-Kohen (1650-1723), had settled in Neiderwerren, near Munich where Benjamin's father, Menachen Kohnstamm, was born about 1762. Kohnstamm emigrated to England in 1782, settled in Brighton in that year, married Hannah Benjamin, daughter of one of the residents, and anglicized his name to Emanuel Hyam Cohen. By all accounts, he was the religious leader of Brighton's small Jewish community, which had no rabbi. He established a school, teaching Hebrew and German for many years until 1816. He was the *shochet* who provided his community with kosher meat. When Brighton's small synagogue was dissolved in 1813, he worked single-handedly to have it revived, an effort which proved successful by 1821, two years before his death.[2]

Emanuel and Hannah Cohen had 12 children. Their first son, Levy Emanuel, born in 1796, was a credit to his father. At age 13 he was a prodigy and taught in his father's school. In 1821, when his father's synagogue was formally reconstituted, he joined it as secretary as well as reader. After his father's death in 1823 he undertook responsibility for bringing up the family.

Levy Emanuel Cohen was no supporter of the *status quo*.[3] In 1827 he founded the Brighton *Guardian*, and used his newspaper to support social change. Its editorials attacked the Corn Laws, demanded universal suffrage, emphasized that poverty was the cause of crime, praised the 1830 revolution in France, and recommended a political union of the middle classes with the working class, not the aristocracy. In August 1830 a hostile mob broke the windows of his newspaper office and hanged him in effigy as the result of his editorial comment that "the King is not a strong-minded man."

Benjamin's older brother Levi Emanuel Cohen (1796-1860),
founder and editor of the Brighton Guardian.

Though surrounded by controversy, Cohen did not fear the conse-quences. In November 1832 his report in the Brighton *Guardian* on "incendiary fires" in the areas of Arundel and Horsham led to his conviction for libel "tending to bring the Magistrates of Sussex into contempt, to set the lower classes against the higher and to incite people to acts of incendiarism." Cohen had defended himself with great dignity but the jury of ten men took only a quarter of an hour to find him guilty.[4] On 31 July 1833 he was sentenced to six months' imprisonment at Chelmsford Prison, which was thought to be far enough away to impede the continuity of his newspaper. But Cohen was unrepentant. He continued his weekly editorials from the Chelmsford Gaol. Cohen's incarceration brought the issue of freedom of the press to national attention. On 21 February 1834 the House of Commons debated Cohen's case, but the government refused to take a position and a motion to support his release was defeated 58 votes to 27.

Levy Cohen's position was ultimately vindicated. He built up the Brighton *Guardian's* circulation to over 60,000 and remained editor for the rest of his life. He was twice, from 1841 to 1843, elected president of the Newspaper Society of England, the organization of proprietors of the provincial press. Though he never married and became a recluse in his later life, Cohen remained a committed Jew until his death in 1860.

Emanuel and Hannah Cohen's second son, Moses, was born 15 April 1799. Like his older brother Levy Emanuel, Moses showed his independence, but he chose a different path to prove himself. By 1822, the year before his father died, he had left Brighton, taking up residence in Liverpool. He had changed his name to George Benjamin, adopting his mother's maiden name as his surname.[5] Even more of a break with tradition, he had joined the Orange order — a secret society devoted to maintaining the dominance of Protestantism over Roman Catholicism in Ireland and elsewhere. Whatever attraction the Orange order held for George Benjamin, his Jewish religion did not seem to be an obstacle to his membership.

It is known that he "was engaged in commercial pursuits" while in Liverpool, and that he travelled extensively.[6] He learned to speak half a dozen languages.[7] The rest of this period of his life remains a mystery, although there is no doubt he received considerable training as a newspaperman, probably from his older brother Levy. Indeed, other brothers and sisters received the same training. His younger brother Abraham Cohen, who moved to Australia in 1835, is known to have worked as a printer at the Sydney *Guardian* and a year later to have become part-owner and publisher of the *Australian*.[8]

George Benjamin had left England some time after his father's death in 1823, possibly in 1829 when his younger brother Benjamin left for Philadelphia. He settled in the American South — he told everyone he had lived in North Carolina — and, in 1832, married Isabella Jacobs, who had been born in New Orleans, not quite 13 years before.[9]

Somewhere along the way Benjamin had developed the idea that his abilities could be used best as a public servant — an idea that could not yet be fully achieved in England. He was likely influenced by the example of his uncle, Hyam Lewis, the first Jew to hold municipal office in England. Born in Prague, Lewis (1769-1851) settled in Brighton about 1790, carried on business as a silversmith and pawnbroker, and was made a citizen in 1816.[10] He became the first Jew to hold elected municipal office in England when he was elected to, and took his seat as, an improvement commissioner of Brighthelmstone in 1822, fully eight years before the next recorded example of a Jew being elected to municipal office.[11] It is a measure of his renown at this time that he was depicted on

Benjamin's uncle, Hyam Lewis (c. 1769-1851).
When he was elected as an improvement commissioner
for Brighthelmstone in 1822, he became the first elected
municipal politician in England.

a print of "Lewis and Brighton," published and distributed by a known artist.[12] Lewis had been previously elected to public office as an improvement commissioner in 1814, but had not been qualified to take office at that time. He was an observant Jew, a member of London's Great Synagogue, and served as elder and president of the Brighton Synagogue.[13] There is no doubt that Benjamin followed Lewis' political career with great interest.

"Lewis and Brighton" by Richard Dighton, 1826.

Jews had, as a group, been expelled from England in 1290. Although they were allowed back in 1656, during the time of Cromwell's Commonwealth, they returned as aliens, lacking not only English citizenship but also the civil and political rights that most Englishmen could take for granted. By the time George Benjamin left England for America, most Jews in England had acquired rights of citizenship, but political rights were still not available to them. In England, Jews could not sit in Parliament unless they were willing to swear the oath of abjuration, attesting that ("on my true faith as a Christian") they did not accept the Catholic descendants of the Pretender, King James III, as having a claim to the throne of England. Jews could not hold office in any municipal corporation (or other corporation for that matter) because the Test Act of 1673[14] required them to receive the "Sacrament of the Lord's Supper" according to the usages of the Church of England after divine service on a Sunday within one month of their appointment. The Test Act applied to the holders of many other government offices as well.[15] Roman Catholics, who suffered from similar disabilities, were finally given complete relief by the British Parliament under the Catholic Emancipation Act of 1829. But Jews in England were obliged to wait up to 30 years longer.

In 1828, intending to give some relief to non-Anglicans, Parliament had passed a statute waiving the requirement of the sacrament for all officers in the army below the rank of major general and in the navy below the rank of rear admiral.[16] Similarly, the sacrament was no longer to be a qualification for office holders in the government departments of revenue, post office, or customs. But the statute required all other government officers and persons elected to municipal office to swear "on the true faith of a Christian" that they would uphold the Anglican Church. In 1836, for example, when David Salomons, a Jew, was elected sheriff of London he was unable to take office until a special act of Parliament was passed dispensing with the oath requirement in his case.[17] Henry Solomon, George Benjamin's brother-in-law, had already been made chief constable of Brighton, which was not an incorporated municipality, in 1829. The same act that allowed David Salomons to become sheriff was used to allow Henry Solomon to be appointed first chief constable of Brighton when it became incorporated in 1838.[18] Near the end of 1836, when David Salomons was elected alderman for the City of London, he was unable to take office again because of the oath requirement. It was not until after 1845, when Parliament passed a law removing the oath requirement for officers of municipal corporations, that Salomons was able to assume office.

Henry Solomon (c. 1794-1844), Brighton's chief constable, married Benjamin's sister Martha.

When Baron Lionel de Rothschild was elected to the House of Commons in 1847, he was unable to take his seat without swearing as a Christian. Again, David Salomons, the London alderman, was forced to wait, without being able to take his seat, when he was elected to the commons in 1851. It was not until 23 July 1858 that Rothschild was finally seated as a member after being continuously elected over a period of 11 years.

Upper Canada must have appeared to George Benjamin as the place to be. It combined the best of the traditions of loyalty and attachment to the British crown with the freedom and individual liberty of the American frontier. The province was new and developing. Since 1830 it had experienced an economic boom and an enormous wave of immigration. The population of Toronto alone had more than tripled in four years.

The Anglican church was established as the official church of the province, even though Methodists and members of other forms of American Protestantism were fast becoming a majority. For one reason or another, by the time of the Benjamins' arrival, the conservative-minded group in control of the colonial government was in the process of removing all disabilities for Jewish office holders — a process that was moving much more slowly in the mother country.

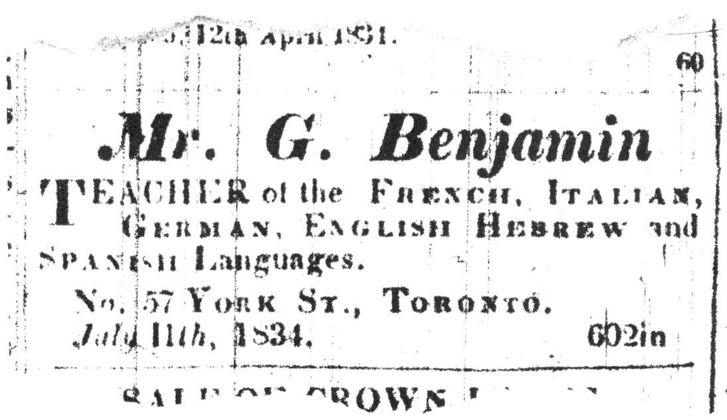

Benjamin's advertisement in the local press appeared in the
Patriot and Farmers Monitor *in Toronto on 18 July 1834.*

On 11 July 1834 George Benjamin announced his presence in Toronto through an advertisement in the local press. "Mr. G. Benjamin," the notice ran, "TEACHER of the FRENCH, ITALIAN, GERMAN, ENGLISH HEBREW and SPANISH Languages" was at 57 York Street,

Toronto.[19] The Benjamins, however, did not stay long in Toronto. The city's hustle and bustle was undoubtedly attractive. It had just been formed out of the town of York and the surrounding countryside, increasing its population from about 6,000 souls to more than 9,000. But whether because of the difficulties of starting up a private practice as a language teacher, or whether it was because of a new opportunity that presented itself, George Benjamin decided to move out of Toronto within only a month or two of announcing his presence.

For one thing, Benjamin had been invited to move to Belleville by James Hunter Sampson.[20] Sampson, about the same age as Benjamin, was in Toronto representing Hastings County in the House of Assembly, a position he had held since 1828. Benjamin and Sampson shared a common political outlook as well as an understanding that the established order needed to be defended against those who would "clog the wheels of government" in "a party spirit."[21] Sampson lived in Belleville, a town of about 1,000 souls just over a 100 miles to the east, and the largest settlement between Toronto and Kingston.

Belleville was of interest to Benjamin for another reason. If he had wanted to follow a career in journalism, as had his older brother Levy in Brighton, he would have undoubtedly investigated Belleville. Toronto already had six newspapers.[22] Belleville had none. Three newspapers had failed in succession, starting as far back as 1831. By mid 1834, the third of these, the *Standard of Moira*, had failed after only a month of operation.[23] Its printing presses, all assembled and ready for operation, were up for sale.[24]

Belleville lay below the rolling hills of Hastings County on the east side of the Moira River, near its opening into the Bay of Quinte on the north shore of Lake Ontario. A traveller coming from Toronto would first have reached the west bank of the Moira and seen Belleville framed against a blue sky across the river. Although the setting was beautiful, the general impression of the town itself was one of drabness. The Moira was a raging torrent in early spring but by summer it slowed to a trickle. There was an old wooden bridge, built 25 years earlier, that led across to join the east bank and entered the town on Bridge Street, where it joined Front Street at the main intersection. Front Street, which ran north and south along

Belleville, looking east along Bridge Street, c. 1830, showing the building at the north-east corner of Front and Bridge Streets that Benjamin's Intelligencer *would soon occupy.*

the river, was the settlement's main commercial street, but its buildings were all of wood and only four of those showed traces of paint. There were no sidewalks or drains, dust was kicked up by teams of horses, and mudholes remained even on dry days. A block further south, Front joined Dundas Street, the main road out of town to the east. Dundas ran along the crest of an escarpment that allowed a long view of the Bay of Quinte to the south. It was here, as one would expect, that some of the larger residences were built. The rest of the town, laid out on regular lots with little apparent order, filled in the area north of Dundas and east of Front. There were a few brick and stone houses, but only two of them had more than one storey. There was one brick church — St Thomas' — and a frame building used by the Methodists.[25]

Belleville was not incorporated, but was simply a settlement that formed part of Thurlow Township. The whole area was experiencing good times, and was quickly being settled by farmers, mostly Protestants, from Ireland. Hastings, in which Belleville was located, was not a county in the modern sense of the word. It was simply an area set up for land registration and some minor court functions. It was composed of 24 townships laid out in 8 rows of 3, stretching north from the Bay of Quinte. The three townships on the bay — the "front townships" they were called — included Sidney, Thurlow, and Tyendinaga. These townships had most of the population and almost all of the prosperity. The next row north, containing the townships of Rawdon, Huntingdon, and Hungerford, had a small population. There were a few settlers in the townships of Marmora, Madoc, and Elzevir, the next row to the north. The remaining townships to the north were uninhabited.

There was no county town, and the entire county, for administrative purposes, was part of the Midland District, headquartered in Kingston. But times were changing and it was becoming evident that soon Hastings would be its own administrative district, and Belleville its district town.

When Sampson suggested the Benjamins should move to Belleville, George Benjamin took up the invitation. In September 1834, for the second time in two months, Benjamin notified the public that he had opened a new business. His "Prospectus" advised the public that he had "taken possession of the Press at Belleville" and was to be the editor and publisher of a newspaper under the name of the *Belleville Intelligencer and Hastings General Advertiser*.[26]

The sudden shift to the newspaper business was as logical as it was significant: it connected with Benjamin's past as well as his future. The prospects of a newspaperman in Upper Canada were excellent if the newspaper could strike a responsive chord among its readers. The newspaper was a method of mass communication in a day when word of mouth and the letter were the only alternatives. Throughout the countryside, people awaited the arrival of the weekly paper and gave its contents and concepts sustained attention — usually in groups. One account will suffice:

> Generally on the evening after the paper comes to hand, a few of the neighbours assemble in my house, and after our homely compliments are exchanged a *reader* is appointed, who, after drawing a chair up to the table, trimming the candle, and clearing his throat,

unceremoniously bawls out, "Silence" — and immediately all are attention. After the reading is over, then come the remarks.[27]

The editor and publisher of such a paper was more than a spreader of news and a leader of opinion. The personal style of the colonial newspaper meant that the bearer of news, as much as the subjects of the reports, would take on a personality that grew with the paper's acceptance. The editor and publisher of an established newspaper, in short, would become an important public figure.

The connection of the newspaper business with Benjamin's past was clear, although an element of mystery surrounded him. From the outset, the *Intelligencer* notified the public that Benjamin was its printer as well as its publisher.[28] It was not unusual for a person to enter the business as a publisher or editor without experience, but printing was a separate trade. To be a printer of a newspaper without some form of apprenticeship was unheard of. Benjamin may have had contact with journalism and printing through his brother Levy Emanuel Cohen, although it is also possible that he had left Brighton long before 1828, when the Brighton *Guardian* was founded. Somewhere in his travels, Benjamin had learned the newspaper business. Its potential was enormous. He could become established in a new country. He could be recognized as a leader of men. He would be seen for what he was.

Benjamin's medal, Loyal Orange Order, Liverpool,
12 July 1822.

NOTES

1 The authors are greatly indebted to David Spector of Hove, England, for making his research available as well as for providing photographs of contemporary drawings. The authors are also indebted to the Cohen family descendants in England (particularly Anne Marx and her husband Theodore) for genealogical information.

2 David Spector, "The Jews of Brighton, 1770-1900," *Jewish Historical Society of England Transactions*, XXII (1970), pp. 42-52. *See also* Cecil Roth, *The rise of provincial Jewry* (London, The Jewish Monthly, 1950), pp. 34-39.

3 Information obtained from David Spector's article "Brighton Jewry reconsidered" (mss.), pp. 7-9, based on a lecture delivered to the Jewish Historical Society of England in 1987. The authors are indebted to David Spector for supplying a copy of the article prior to its publication in *Jewish Historical Society of England Transactions*.

4 *See* the "Speech of the Defendant, Levy Emanuel Cohen, at the TRIAL 'The King v. Cohen'" in the Brighton *Guardian*, 28 November 1860, reprinted in the *Jewish Chronicle*.

5 George Benjamin was known as "Mo" to his family and signed his letters to them in that manner: Abraham Cohen family papers in the possession of Henry Robert Cohen, Mossman, New South Wales. George and Isabella Benjamin's grandchildren were aware that Moses was a family name although it appears, erroneously, as the name of George Benjamin's father in "George C. Benjamin's family record, 1914," p. 2, Benjamin family papers. This record is an account written in 1914 by Benjamin's daughter-in-law Henrietta Cote (widow of Louis Nathan Benjamin) for her son George C. Benjamin.

6 "George Benjamin," *Appleton's cyclopaedia of American biography*, vol. I, James Grant Wilson and John Fiske, eds. (New York, D. Appleton and Company, 1887).

7 See *Patriot and Farmers' Monitor* (Toronto, Thomas Dalton, publisher), 18 July 1834, p. 3. According to Moodie, *op. cit.*, p. 482, he "has been to all parts of the world and speaks half a dozen languages." "George Benjamin File," Hastings County Historical Society collection, item no. 2385, Belleville Public Library.

8 Abraham Cohen family papers in the possession of Henry Robert Cohen. Summary on file in the Australian Jewish Historical Society, Great Synagogue, Sydney, N. S. W.

9 Mackenzie Bowell, Benjamin's protégé, wrote at the time of Benjamin's death that before coming to Toronto he (Benjamin) had resided in North Carolina. *Intelligencer*, 9 September 1864. On the other hand, a short biography written later states that "In his early manhood he went to New Orleans." *Appleton's cyclopaedia*. *See also* "George C. Benjamin's family record, 1914," p. 3. Benjamin family papers

state that "*George Cohen* alias *George Benjamin* yr. grandfather — He ran away from home to New Orleans La. & took his mother's name so they could not trace him."

[10] David Spector, "The Jews of Brighton, 1770-1900," and his "Brighton Jewry Reconsidered," *Jewish Historical Society of England Transactions*, XXX (1987-88), pp. 91-124.

[11] This is the conclusion of David Spector in "The Jews of Brighton" at p. 46 and "Brighton Jewry Reconsidered" at p. 97. The conclusion is reinforced by reference to James Picciotto, *Sketches of Anglo Jewish History* (London, 1875) (Reprinted: London, Soncino Press, 1956), pp. 390, 484. Picciotto, who was unaware of Hyam Lewis, concluded that "Mr Phineas Levi of Devonport was the first Jew who held municipal office in England." Levi was a member of the Devonport Board of Commissioners in 1830.

[12] "LEWIS and BRIGHTON" by Richard Dighton, 1826. *See* Dennis Rose, *Life times and recorded works of Robert Dighton (1752-1814) actor, artist and printseller and thence of his artist sons* (Lewes, 1981), p. 44.

[13] Cecil Roth, *The Rise of provincial Jewry* (London, The Jewish Monthly, 1950), p. 39.

[14] 25 Charles II, c. 2 (1673).

[15] For a general review of this subject see Henry Strauss Quixano Henriques, *Jews and the English law* (Oxford University Press, 1908). This work was reprinted from a series of 11 articles published in the *Jewish Quarterly Review* between 1901 and 1907. In particular, see "The Political Rights of English Jews," part I, XIX (1907), pp. 298-341 and part II, XIX (1907), pp. 751-91. The authors are in the process of completing a work on the development of civil and political rights by Jews in the British North American context during the century after 1750.

[16] 8 George IV, c. 17 (1828).

[17] 5 and 6 William IV, c. 28 (1836).

[18] Spector, "The Jews of Brighton," p. 45 and "Brighton Jewry Reconsidered," p. 28. Henry Solomon (b. *c.* 1794) was tragically murdered in his office by a youth who had been arrested for stealing a carpet, leaving his widow, Benjamin's sister Martha, and ten children.

[19] See note 7 *supra*.

[20] Gerald E. Boyce, "James Hunter Sampson," *Dictionary of Canadian Biography*, vol. VII. Sampson had moved to Belleville after his call to the bar in 1823, becoming Belleville's first lawyer.

[21] The *Chronicle and Gazette* (Kingston), 30 August 1834, quoting George Benjamin's "Prospectus" for the *Belleville Intelligencer and Hastings General Advertiser*.

[22] E. G. Firth, *The town of York 1815-1834* (Toronto, Champlain Society, University of Toronto Press, 1966), population statistics at p. lxxxii, information on newspapers at p. 356.

[23] *Anglo Canadian*, founded by Alexander James Williamson (February 1831 to June 1831); *Phoenix*, founded by Thomas Slicer (June 1831 to 3 July 1832); and *Hastings Times and Farmers' Journal*, founded by Rollin C. Benedict (3 July 1832 to 11 May 1833). *Standard of Moira* appeared in 1834 but lasted only from 26 June to 21 July. *See* typescript article by William H. Cooper as introduction to mfm of Belleville newspapers, accession no. 6806 at the PAO (6 August 1970). *See also Inventory of Ontario Newspapers, 1793-1986*, comp. and ed. J. B. Gilchrist (Toronto, Micromedia, 1987).

[24] P. L. Fleming, *Upper Canadian imprints, 1801-1841: a bibliography* (Toronto, University of Toronto Press, 1988), appendix A: "Newspapers," Elizabeth Hulse, comp., p. 422, n. 5. Benjamin had stated in his "Prospectus" that he had "taken possession of the Press at Belleville." Hulse notes that this was "presumably the press of the defunct *Standard of Moira*." On 26 June 1834 the *Standard of Moira* had issued its first number and on 31 July its last. *Ibid.*, pp. 421-22, n. 4.

[25] *See* Nick and Helma Mika, *Mosaic of Belleville* (Belleville, Mika Silk Screening Limited, 1966), pp. 22-32.

[26] Benjamin's "Prospectus."

[27] William Kilbourn, *The firebrand* (Toronto, Clarke Irwin, 1956), p. 33.

[28] "Newspapers," Hulse, p. 422, n. 5.

CHAPTER III

The Challenge

"Oh ladies all and gentlemen,
While I've nothing else to do,
I'll just sit down and sing a song
About the Belleville Jew."

British Whig, *Kingston, 27 April 1836*

THE KINGSTON NEWSPAPER LAY SPREAD ON THE DESK IN FRONT OF THE window. George Benjamin stood before it, without his coat, his checked shirt, not over clean, tucked up to his elbows. His smile, gone as if dropped from his face. His colour, drained.[1] Mackenzie Bowell, his apprentice and a lad of about 14, who had just brought in the paper with the rest of the day's mail, shifted uncomfortably as he watched his employer.[2] They stood at the front of a long, low loft, two storeys above the street. At the rear, a large printing press, its galleys filled with type, waited. In the area in between, what appeared at first glance to be clutter proved on closer examination to be evidence of a highly organized enterprise. There were rows of cabinets with shallow drawers, each containing lead type in an amazing array of styles and shapes, arranged in order. There were stacks of papers, some printed, some blank. There were wooden tables, as well as a few chairs. Near the press at the back of the loft, racks against the wall held bottles of printers' ink, and a large variety of equipment not identifiable by the untrained.[3]

Down the long stairs to the landing and down again to the street, life went on as usual. It was at the corner of Front and Bridge streets, the

THE INTELLIGENCER

OF BELLEVILLE, AND HASTINGS GENERAL ADVERTISER.

VOL. I.]　　　BELLEVILLE, U. C. SATURDAY, OCTOBER 11, 1834.　　　[NO. 5.

First page of the Intelligencer, *11 October 1834.*

town's main intersection, facing west. In fact, this building was the first thing a traveller from Toronto would see as he came over the bridge. Over the doorway, a large sign proclaimed that this was the office of the *Intelligencer*, George Benjamin, proprietor.[4] The door itself was remarkable. In a town where painted wooden buildings were the exception rather than the rule, George Benjamin's door was painted black. One of his detractors described it as "a black, ugly, forbidding looking door."[5]

It was Friday morning, 28 April 1836.

Benjamin's mind undoubtedly ran back to the previous Saturday. When he had arrived at his office that morning to distribute the *Intelligencer* — it was published every Saturday — he had found a crowd gathered outside his door. But those assembled had not all come to pick up their papers. From a post in front of the office, a fat dummy hung, a rope about its neck. The dummy was clearly intended to be Benjamin, but those responsible for the joke had done their work during the night and could not be identified. The word was that the hanging in effigy was retribution for Benjamin's strong editorial against the organizing by the "Tee-totallers," but no one could be certain.[6] Soon after the blacksmith came by, reached the dummy with a pole, and took it down. The crowd was friendly — Benjamin had lots of friends — and the incident seemed ended.

Now, scarcely a week later, Dr John Edward Barker, editor and publisher of the Kingston *British Whig*, had carried the matter a step further. Barker had been born in England in 1799, the same year as George Benjamin. Trained as a physician, he had remained in England until 1832, when he arrived in Kingston with his wife. In February 1834, just six months before Benjamin had launched the *Intelligencer*, Barker had given up the practice of medicine and had established the *British Whig* as a vigorous proponent of reform in Upper Canada.[7] Benjamin's unflinching defence of the Conservative order made him a logical target for Barker's sarcasm.

The *Whig* used the report of the incident of Benjamin's hanging in effigy as the basis for a poem which it called "Elegy on the Execution of the Belleville Jew." By almost any standard, the poem was scurrilous. It suggested that it would be no loss if Benjamin were to be hanged. It called his newspaper a "Smut-machine." Worse, it attacked Benjamin for not only being born a Jew, but for being a "snarling hypocrite." It referred to him as "Benjie," as the "Saintly Belleville Jew" who may have died more from eating pork than from any hanging. In the words of the refrain, "For Pork's the meat Jews must not eat, No doubt it killed the Jew."

There was no doubt Benjamin did not follow most of the religious traditions of the Jewish people. There is little doubt, either, that the family of Isabella Jacobs, his wife, had not followed strict religious observance

in New Orleans. An account of that city, written in 1842, had noted that
of 700 Jewish families, only 4 kept a kosher table and only 2 observed
Saturday as Sabbath.[8]

THE BRITISH WHIG.

—OPIFER PER ORBEM-DICOR.—

THURSDAY MORNING, APRIL 27th, 1837.

NEWS FROM BELLEVILLE.

DREADFUL EXECUTION.—At an early hour on the morning of the 22d inst. the body of the Belleville Jew was found suspended by the neck in front of the Intelligencer Office, in effigy! The verdict of the "*Coroner's Inquest*" not yet ascertained

ELEGY

On the Execution of the Belleville Jew.

Oh ladies all and gentlemen,
  While I've nothing else to do,
I'll just sit down and sing a song
  About the Belleville Jew.

Last Friday night some wicked boys
  Thought they would something do :
So they turned out and wheel'd about,
  And hung the Belleville Jew!

Tee-totallers in meeting met,
  Brought Benjies wrath to view ;
They raved and tore, and almost swore
  About the Belleville Jew.

Amid the fray was Preacher K——.
  Whose words were far from few,
Who said the Belleville Smut-machine
  Spoke nothing that was true.

Jew Benjie then to get revenge,
  Did raise a cry and hew
Of Maw-worm, snarling hypocrite,
  Oh ! Saintly Belleville Jew.

Now when the people of the town
  The Smut-machine read through,
They tore the slime and said 'twas time
  To hang the Belleville Jew!

Now no one knows who made the clothes,
  There's nothing but this clue :
That *Mr. Word—on* stitch'd the cord on
  The coat that clad the Jew.

No doubt of that, he swears it flat,
  He made the "LONG TAILED BLUE"
That covered o'er, behind, before
  The body of the Jew.

Bellevillians all both great and small
  Ask who the job did do,
On pestle rod who hung the clod
  Of smutty Belleville Jew.

The MAYOR'S CLERK by way of lark
  Some say did lead the crew,
While others say without delay
  'Twas PORK, and DONT-KNOW-WHO.

Let's stop to pause a double cause
  To show this guessing true,
For PORK's the meat Jews must not eat
  No doubt it killed the Jew.

But oh ! my eyes ! 'tis all surmise—
  The rope what hangman drew,
That brought to shameful sacrifice
  The slandering Belleville Jew.

The neck and brains were hung in chains,
  And would have swung till two,
Had not a smith with pole forthwith
  Pulled down the Belleville Jew.

But now my song has got so long
  Something else will do,
I'll quit until the next smut-mill
  The mystery brings to view.

Something Graphic.—The following letter was written some time since by a boy in Indiana, to his father in New Orleans :

"Dear daddy;—Corn is dull, brother John is dead likewise. Excuse haste in a bad pain. Yours omnipotent,
    John McClure."

"On the Execution of the Belleville Jew"

26

Dr Edward John Barker (1799-1884).
According to his biographer, the editor and publisher of
Kingston's British Whig *"used sarcasm and ridicule with*
devastating skill – often unjustly."

The editor of the *British Whig* would have had even more ammunition if he had known about Benjamin's practice of registering family information on the end-papers of his leather-bound Hebrew prayer-book. But was Benjamin a hypocrite? Did he not consider that he was still Jewish, even though he kept it to himself? Outwardly, George Benjamin lived in a manner that made his family indistinguishable from their Christian neighbours. But inwardly, he drew a line between what he was, a Jew, and what he felt he had to appear to be in order to be fully accepted. Although he may have had to appear like his Christian neighbours, he was still a Jew. Using his Hebrew prayer-book was a symbolic act, to be sure, but it was an act of self-definition. It helped him draw the line. He was no hypocrite. He was doing the best he could under the circumstances. Like the Maranos of Spain,[9] he was following a tradition of trying to blend in as quickly as possible, to gain acceptance and achieve equality in a new land, while secretly maintaining his own links with his religion.

It was just Friday. There was still time for Benjamin to write a counterattack, change the galleys, and still publish the *Intelligencer* on time on Saturday morning.

Mac Bowell, Benjamin's helper, was waiting for his decision. Shortly after they had arrived in Belleville, the Benjamins had taken in Mac, then a motherless immigrant child of about 12. As one of Benjamin's daughters later recalled, Mac "made himself useful around the house and especially in the print shop."[10] Benjamin supported him, saw to his education, and treated him as a son. Over the years, Bowell would become, progressively, Benjamin's employee, business associate, protégé, and closest political ally. Sixty years later, long after Benjamin's death, Mackenzie Bowell, senator, would become Canada's fifth prime minister.[11]

WANTED.

AN Intelligent lad as an Apprentice at this Office.

Job Printing,

In all its branches neatly executed at this Office.

Mackenzie Bowell, later Canada's fifth prime minister,
responded to Benjamin's advertisement in the newspaper.

If Benjamin had thought about it he would have realized that he had achieved an enormous amount in the two short years he had been in Belleville. Not four months earlier he had scored a remarkable electoral triumph. On 4 January 1836, at the annual Thurlow Township meeting in the Belleville court-house, Benjamin ran for the office of clerk (or chairman) of the township, which included Belleville. A vote by show of hands gave Benjamin 69 votes to 68 for Dr Anson Hayden of Hayden's Corners. After a written ballot was demanded, both candidates rounded up additional supporters and the final vote gave Benjamin the clerkship by a count of 144 to 122.

The victory of such a recent arrival was strong evidence of the confidence in which Benjamin was held by the community. But it was more than that. Benjamin had made no secret of his religion. The previous summer, he had been listed as one of the members who donated to the fund for the new synagogue building in Montreal.[12] Benjamin must have been aware of how unusual it was for a Jew to be elected to public office. In fact, his election as clerk was the first recorded instance of a Jew being elected to municipal office in British North America. A month later, Benjamin had added another office to his list of achievements. On 18 February 1836 Lieutenant Governor Francis Bond Head granted him a commission as a notary public entitled to swear oaths.[13] This was the first such recorded appointment of a Jew by a Canadian government, although Eleazar Levy of Quebec had received a similar appointment by imperial commission from Britain, 70 years earlier.[14]

If Benjamin was to think back past 1836, probably the most important thing he had done since he arrived in town was the launching of the *Intelligencer* in September 1834.[15] Its motto called for a contented populace. "Let there be harmony in things essential," it ran, "Liberality in things not essential, Charity in all." Benjamin's prospectus had promised "to be just and advantageous alike to the governed and governing." If men are anxious to shine as political writers," he wrote "let them adopt a fair, honest course for the welfare of the public."[16] Notwithstanding its professed independence, the *Intelligencer* was labelled as conservative by others.[17] Benjamin's eloquence and cutting humour were used to give public support for his views on a wide range of issues. He opposed free trade with the United States, which he felt would hurt Canadian farmers, saying "it is a charming name because it tends to seduce reflection and attention. It is anything but free trade, unless that be called free which gains riches to one and ruin and poverty to the other."[18] He supported Lieutenant Governor Head's resistance to the notions of responsible government raised by the Executive Council led by Robert Baldwin. He called Marshall Spring Bidwell, the radical speaker of the assembly, "a master spirit of mischief."[19] By 1836 the editor of Kingston's *British Whig* had noted that Benjamin did not tolerate observations by outsiders on the political affairs of Hastings "as he regards that field as entirely his own."[20]

Although the Kingston *Chronicle and Gazette* had given the *Intelligencer* only six months to live, it had survived. Benjamin had become one of the leading journalists in the province and was frequently quoted by other papers. While no one at the time knew it, the *Intelligencer* would continue to survive, standing, over 150 years later, as Ontario's oldest operating newspaper.

But all that mattered to George Benjamin that day, as he stood in the *Intelligencer* office planning what to do, was that the slander be forgotten. He folded up the paper and went on with his work.[21]

RAGS received in payment for papers at this Office.

The Intelligencer of Belleville
Is printed and published every Saturday Morning, by GEORGE BENJAMIN at his office, corner of Front and Bridge Streets.

TERMS.

NOTES

[1] Taken from Susanna Moodie's description of Benjamin, pp. 483-84.

[2] The Kingston newspaper of Thursday morning, 27 April 1836, would likely have been received by Benjamin the following morning. Belleville, on the "Grand Canada Mail Route" between Quebec and Toronto, was entitled to "The Eastern Mail, due daily, except Mondays." *See* the article "Post Office" in the *York commercial directory, street guide and register, 1833-4*, comp. George Walton, pp. 137-42, at p. 141.

3 The description again is from Moodie, supplemented by a visit to the office of the *Constitution*, operated as a weekly newspaper in Toronto by William Lyon Mackenzie and reconstructed to 1836 by the Toronto Historical Board at 36 Bond Street.

4 Again, Moodie's description. The sign no longer exists. The wording has been copied from the masthead of the *Intelligencer* of 1836.

5 Moodie, p. 483.

6 The account in this and subsequent paragraphs is based on the "News from Belleville," *British Whig*, Thursday morning, 27 April 1836, p. 3, col. 3.

7 Fleming, p. 430, n. 52. J. W. Spurr, "Edward John Barker," *Dictionary of Canadian Biography*, vol. XI. Barker, according to his biographer, "used sarcasm and ridicule with devastating skill — often unjustly."

8 Max J. Kohler, "Judah P. Benjamin: statesman and jurist," *Publications, American Jewish Historical Society*, 12 (1904), pp. 63-85, at pp. 68-69.

9 According to the *Jewish Encyclopedia*, "Marano (*plural Maranos, generally written Marranos*): Crypto-Jews of the Iberian Peninsula ... . The name was applied to the Spanish Jews who, through compulsion or for form's sake, became converted to Christianity in consequence of the cruel persecutions of 1391 ... who yielded through stress of circumstances, but in their home life remained Jews ... ." Morris A. Gutstein, *The story of the Jews of Newport* (New York, Bloch Publishing Co., 1936), p. 60 states: "Some of the Marranos intermarried with families of the higher and lower nobility to such an extent that after a few generations very few families in Spain were without Jewish blood. They took part in all forms of political and social life. Economically they acquired wealth and at times were entrusted with the financial policies of the country. In the royal Court and Chancery, the Marranos occupied many positions in many capacities. They became high dignitaries in the Catholic Church, to the extent that at one time the rumor arose that a Marrano had reached the position of Pope."

10 "The Birth of a Paper," *Intelligencer*, 24 June 1924, Hastings County Historical Society Collection, no. 748, Belleville Public Library.

11 Mackenzie Bowell, son of John Bowell, was born at Suffolk, England, on 27 December 1823, came to Canada in 1833, and shortly after obtained employment as "printer's devil," apprenticed to George Benjamin at the *Intelligencer* in Belleville. In 1847 he married Harriet Louise (d. 1884), daughter of Jacob G. Moore of Belleville, and sister of Rodney Moore, printer of the *Intelligencer*. He was first elected to the House of Commons as a Conservative representing North Hastings in 1867 and represented that constituency continuously until 1892, when he has appointed to the Senate. In 1878, as minister of customs in the government led by Sir John A. Macdonald, he was responsible for the implementation of the National Policy. On the death of Sir John Thompson in 1894 Bowell became prime minister of Canada. Knighted in 1895, he resigned as prime minister on 27 April 1896

after half his ministers, "a nest of traitors" Bowell called them, had resigned in a body the previous January. He retired from the Senate in 1906 and died in Belleville on 10 December 1917. *Macmillan Dictionary of Canadian Biography*, ed. W. Stewart Wallace, fourth edition, rev. by W. A. McKay (Toronto, Macmillan of Canada, 1978), pp. 88-89.

[12] Gerald E. Boyce, *Historic Hastings* (Belleville, Hastings County Council, 1967), p. 52.

[13] Benjamin Hart, Moses Judah Hayes, and Isaac Valentine, "To our Brethren in Israel in the United States and British North America," *Canadian Jewish Archives, new series*, no. 28 (Montreal, Canadian Jewish Congress, 1983), pp. 45-46. The list indicated that "George Benjamin, Montreal," who donated $20, was one of 31 contributors.

[14] "List of Public Notaries for Upper Canada," PAO, RG53, 66, vol. 1. *See also* F. A. Armstrong, *A handbook of Upper Canada chronology* (revised edition, Toronto, Dundurn Press, 1985), p. 132.

[15] Eleazar Levy (c. 1716-1811) arrived in Quebec from New York in May 1760 and moved on to Montreal by 1763. He received an imperial commission as a notary on 24 December 1766, and was allowed to delete the words "in Christ" from his application. *See* NAC, RG68, liber C, part B, imperial commissions, pp. 31 and 32; and L3, I 13, vol. 1, pp. 185-86. *See also* Edgar Roy Samuel, "Anglo-Jewish Notaries and Scriveners," *Jewish Historical Society of England Transactions*, XVII, pp. 113-59, at pp. 114 and 157.

[16] William H. Cooper, "Introduction," a typescript article at the beginning of the collection of issues of the *Belleville Intelligencer*, accession 6806, N 219, mfm reel 5.

[17] *Kingston Chronicle and Gazette*, 30 August 1834.

[18] *Kingston Chronicle and Gazette*, 29 November 1834.

[19] *British Whig*, 25 June 1836.

[20] *Kingston Chronicle and Gazette*, 4 May 1838.

[21] The conclusion that Benjamin folded up the paper and went on with his work is based on circumstantial evidence. That he ignored the insults follows from Susanna Moodie's comment that, "The people twice hung him in effigy, but that public indignity offered to his person produced no effect. He only laughed at what he termed their impotent revenge." "Richard Redpath," *op. cit.*, p. 483. Again, folding the newspapers of other publishers was usual: papers were delivered folded in the mail or by hand, and were stored folded.

CHAPTER IV

Of Freedom and Acceptance

> "I A. B. do declare that I do believe that there
> is not any transubstantiation in the Sacrament of the Lord's
> Supper or in the elements of bread and wine at or after the
> consecration thereof by any person whatsoever."
>
> *Oath or test administered to officials of Upper Canada from*
> *9 July 1792 to 13 February 1833*

To all intents and purposes, George Benjamin had played the game. He had redoubled his efforts to be accepted. In June 1836, after Belleville had been incorporated as a police village, he was appointed first clerk of its council or Board of Police as well as one of the village's constables. People in Belleville did not care what one of the newspapers in Kingston said about Benjamin.[1] Then, in December 1837, when radicals throughout the province became rebels and led an armed uprising against the established order, Benjamin did his part as one of the government's most active supporters. According to one observer, he was "the prime mover" in exposing those Belleville citizens who were disloyal to the government, as well as ensuring that they were brought to justice.[2]

Benjamin's zeal was acknowledged on 16 February 1838 when he was granted a commission as a captain in the 4th Regiment of Hastings Militia.[3] George Benjamin was not in it for the glory. Only four days later, when a chance came for the 1st Regiment to join the action against the rebels, at age 39 and overweight, he enlisted as a private in Wellington Murney's company.[4] With Benjamin in its ranks, the 1st marched off to Gananoque and captured a band of rebels who had gathered at Hickory

Island in the St Lawrence.[5]

Shortly after Benjamin's march back through Kingston, the *British Whig* struck again. "Mr Benjamin is an English Jew as admitted by himself," the *British Whig* reminded its readers on 11 May, "and yet he has been recently appointed to a captaincy in the Militia. Now by the English law," the editor continued, in a tone that masked his ignorance of the subject, "Jews are not naturalized subjects of the Crown, and can neither hold real estate, sit in Parliament or bear commissions in the Army or Navy . ... Now if Mr. Benjamin is an alien at home, he is an alien in Canada, for no provincial statute takes away his disqualification here and consequently he is unlawfully holding the commission of captain."[6]

The editorial was bursting with inaccuracies.[7] The *British Whig* was an Upper Canadian not a British newspaper, and the colonial laws in force were much further ahead in their liberality than those affecting civil and political rights in the mother country. Even by English law, Jews born in England, such as Benjamin, were British subjects, not aliens. Even Jews born in foreign countries who would be considered aliens if they immigrated to England, could become "naturalized" British subjects if they came to British North America and took the benefit of the Naturalisation Act of 1740.[8]

The right of Jews to hold real estate in British North America was also beyond question. Jews had held land and taken grants from the crown in all the colonies from the time of earliest British settlement. Jewish land owners were accepted by the English when New York was captured from the Dutch in 1663.[9] John Franks, a Jew, continued this tradition when he was granted the first settlement grant in British North America in the Halifax allotment in August 1749.[10] In fact, the only doubt as to the right of Jews to take crown grants in Upper Canada had been put to rest 30 years before the Benjamins' arrival,[11] and no similar doubts had been raised in any of the other colonies of British North America.[12] There were a number of instances of Jews being granted crown land in the 1780s in the portions of the old Province of Quebec that were to become Upper Canada,[13] as well as in the early 1790s in Upper Canada immediately after its formation.[14]

The *British Whig* was wrong too about holding commissions in the army or navy. Jews had been regularly appointed by commission as officers in the militia in both Upper and Lower Canada for many years. The first Jewish officer on record in Canada, Moses David, was made an ensign in the Upper Canada militia before 1803. He was made a captain by 1807 and a lieutenant by 1812.[15]

There had even been Jewish office holders in Upper Canada.[16] What had prevented conscientious Jews from holding some offices was not a "disqualification," as the *British Whig* suggested, but rather the fact that the oath used as a condition of holding office contained words an observant Jew would not swear—words acknowledging Protestant Christianity. In this light, the *British Whig's* statement, "no provincial statute takes away his disqualification here," also missed the mark. In 1833 Upper Canada passed an amendment to its Oaths Act, which removed the remaining Jewish "disability" by substituting a simple form of oath as a qualification for all offices, in place of the Christian oath.[17] The passage of the amendment to the Oaths Act was not an isolated instance. On an official level, the conservative members of the "family compact," or ruling clique that dominated the government of the province, believed that there should be equality of Jewish rights in Upper Canada. "Suppose there were a Congregation of Jews in this town," Attorney General Henry John Boulton had asked the members of the assembly in 1831. "Would they not be entitled to the protection of this House ... as much as any other sect or denomination?"[18]

By the time the Benjamins arrived in Upper Canada, there was no law that prevented a conscientious Jew from holding office, even as a member of the assembly.

It is not known whether or not Benjamin made a public reply to the editor of the *British Whig* because the issues of the *Intelligencer* of the day have not survived. But he had already replied to the attitudes represented by the *British Whig* in a different way. Months earlier he had faced a rebellion directed at him personally, rather than at the province of Upper Canada. As the incident was recalled in the newspaper a week after his death, the drama of the confrontation as well as the strength of Benjamin's response increased his stature. The story was retold as follows:

During the period immediately preceding the outbreak of the rebellion in 1837-38, Mr Benjamin commanded a company of the militia of the township of Sidney, which township was suspected of being rather strongly tinctured with feelings of disaffection toward the government. Either from this or from some other cause, the members of the company resolved to enjoy a sardonic joke at their captain's expense. Mr Benjamin, being short-sighted, habitually wore spectacles, and according to the fashion of the day, occasionally appeared in crimson overalls. One morning when called out for exercise the company mustered with red stockings drawn over their pants, and every man a huge pair of leather spectacles over his nose. Mr Benjamin took no notice of this extraordinary equipment, and proceeded to put them through the customary evolutions, in the course of which he manoeuvred so as to draw them up in line opposite the margin of a frog-hole which he had observed in a part of the field in which they were exercising, and gave the word "quick march!" On arriving at the brink they hesitated, as expecting the command which would stop their further progress, but it did not come, and in they went, up to their knees in the water and slime of the pool. After keeping them long enough in this position to change the laugh to the other side of the face, Captain Benjamin gave the magic words, "Right about face, march," which released them from the cool element, and from their unexpected predicament. The red stockings and the leather spectacles did not make their appearance again on parade.[19]

The story may have been published as a humorous anecdote, but it was no joke to Benjamin and his serious deliberate response lost nothing in the telling. It may have been the strong tincture of feelings of disaffection with the colonial government in the township of Sidney, or it may have been "some other cause," as the storyteller put it — perhaps the disaffection in being led in military manoeuvres by a Jew (certainly a unique experience in Upper Canada), that had made Benjamin's men question his authority. Whatever it was, he had met the challenge and had won. It was he who had known how far to go and it was they who had been pushed over the line.

Benjamin's religion was noticed, although he had chosen not to make the practice of Judaism his priority. No matter what he did, everyone seemed to know he was Jewish, particularly after the *British Whig's* attack of April 1838. In time, the force of his personality would overcome his detractors. But he could accelerate the process if he became more adept than his neighbours at promoting their objectives.

When he had first come to Belleville, he had received a warrant for the establishment of Orange Lodge No. 102 in Thurlow Township — the second such lodge in Upper Canada.[20] Benjamin's participation in an order of this nature was undoubtedly unusual for a Jew. According to the order's objects as adopted at a meeting of its Grand Lodge in Brockville in 1830, it had been "formed by persons desirous of supporting to the utmost of their power, the principles and practice of the Christian religion."[21] Again, according to the order's objects, the members were associating "in honour of King William the III, Prince of Orange, whose name we bear, and whose immortal memory we hold in reverence, tending as he did under Divine Providence, to the overthrow of the most oppressive bigotry, and the restoration of the pure form of Religion and Liberty, established in the British Empire." "We hope," the objects concluded, "in the adoption of his name, to emulate his virtues, by maintaining Religion without persecution or trenching on the rights of any." Though on the surface the Orange institution appeared to be an organization of and for Protestant Christians, its objects contained elements of a new approach towards religious harmony, which a Jew of the early 19th century could actively support. Orangemen preached toleration of minorities by governments. While not mentioned by name in the objects, governments that were dominated by the Roman Catholic Church were seen by Orangemen as the enemies of religious liberty for minorities. William III, Prince of Orange, who had died 130 years earlier, was emulated as one who believed in "maintaining Religion without persecution, or trenching on the rights of any."

For centuries Jews had worked to achieve the same goals, the horrors of the Inquisition burned into their souls. Mark the words of Jacob Henry, a North American Jewish politician about 25 years earlier: "If a man fulfills the duties of that religion, which his education or his conscience has pointed to him as the true one, no person, I hold, in this our land of liberty, has the right to arraign him at the bar of any inquisition: and the day, I trust, has long passed, when principles merely speculative were propagated by force; when the sincere and pious were made victims, and the light-minded bribed into hypocrites."[22] Jacob Henry was from North Carolina where Benjamin had lived. His words could have been Benjamin's.

The popular notion that the driving force of the Orange order was hatred of Catholics is not borne out by the words of its leaders. In their public pronouncements Orangemen took pains to repeat that they did not oppose Catholics, they opposed the perceived control of the Roman Catholic Church over governments in countries where Roman Catholicism was the official religion. They felt that in countries of this nature — "theocracies" they called them — dissenters and adherents of other religions were not tolerated. Orangemen did not oppose toleration for Roman Catholics. They did want to ensure that the Roman Catholic Church would not be given any form of ascendancy in Canada.

In the words of Professor Goldwin Smith, "the sage of the Grange," speaking at the annual parade of Orangemen in Toronto on 12 July 1888, "William III saved Europe and saved the world from falling back into darkness and slavery. (Cheers) At that time Protestantism had been extirpated in France by the sword of Louis XIV, with every circumstance of perfidy and cruelty. The fires of the Inquisition were still then burning. It was a great deliverance, not only for England but for the whole world. (Cheers)."[23] What "Rome wanted was not equality, but domination."[24] He saw the Orange procession as "the exhibition of a safeguard and a guarantee not only for the civil and religious liberties of the Orange Order but the whole nation."[25]

Brother John Ross Robertson, MP, expressed the argument even more strongly when he addressed the annual gathering of the Orange order in Toronto on 12 July 1897. "We love liberty of speech, freedom of conscience and right of action for every man and woman in the land. We abhor despotism in any form whether the work of crafty priests or cunning politician. We demand for ourselves no more than we are willing to grant to others, for the acme of Orangeism is toleration to every color, class or creed and personal freedom for all mankind."[26]

In Benjamin's time, and earlier, European countries with Protestant monarchs had, as a rule, been tolerant of religious minorities, unlike those with Roman Catholic monarchs. Had not Spain and Portugal expelled their Jewish populations more than 300 years earlier and not allowed them to return? Had not France given only the slightest toleration to its Huguenot and Jewish minorities and not allowed them to settle in the French colonies in North America? On the other hand, the Protestant Dutch, led by the first William of Orange, had been tolerant and liberal to the Jews after they secured their independence from Spain in 1575 and established the Netherlands. Jews had been allowed to live in Protestant England for over a century and had been granted equality in many respects.

The Orange institution had no rule that would have barred non-Protestants from membership, but its ceremonies and proceedings would have been objectionable to a conscientious and observant Jew. The prescribed opening prayer, to be said by all members at all lodge meetings, finished with the words "through Jesus Christ Our Lord." The closing prayer concluded "all which we humbly beg for the sake of our blessed Lord and Saviour Jesus Christ." In introducing new candidates to membership, the master of a lodge was required to read several passages from the New Testament, concluding with the words "That we should believe on the name of his Son Jesus Christ, and love one another as he gave us commandment."[27] Though he was not a Christian, George Benjamin was master of Belleville's Orange lodge and, one assumes, was required to say all these prayers. He took the position none the less.

There had certainly been a tradition among Jews of condoning conversion to Christianity to save one's life. So it was with the Maranos or "New Christians" who had been forced to convert during the Spanish and Portuguese inquisitions, yet remained secret Jews. Those who had been fortunate enough to escape to tolerant countries were in many cases welcomed as Jews by their co-religionists.

Was Benjamin practising as a Marano as perhaps his Spanish ancestors, the family of Don Menachen ben Chajim Ha-Kohen, had been in the 16th century? That rationale hardly seemed likely in Benjamin's case. He said Christian prayers, not to save his life, as had his forebearers, but to achieve something that otherwise would have been denied him because of his religion. But then Benjamin would not have been the first to have done that. By saying these words he was not converting to Christianity or taking an oath, he was saying Christian prayers. Ezekiel Hart of Three Rivers had kissed the Holy Gospels in 1809 when he wanted to take his seat in the Lower Canadian Assembly.[28] He was still a Jew. And Hart's son, Aaron Ezekiel, had sworn an oath "on my true faith as a Christian" in order to be enrolled as Canada's first Jewish lawyer in 1823.[29]

Was Benjamin then just a "snarling hypocrite," as the Kingston paper had said? Perhaps, in view of his long family history, he felt that the importance of the objects of the Orange order, rather than the ceremonial words read at meetings, were the priority.

There was one custom that George Benjamin kept that was unequivocally Jewish. When the Benjamins' second child, Esther Eliza, was born on 16 July 1835, her birth was registered by George Benjamin in his leather-bound Hebrew prayer-book, which was kept, for his family, at home. Unlike their Christian neighbours, who kept regular records of births, deaths, and marriages through a formal system of church and parish records, Jews in North America had no formal method of keeping records. Most communities where Jews lived did not have active synagogues, and even where they existed it was rare for records of that nature to be kept. The problem was regarded as so serious by the Jewish community in Montreal that in 1828 a large group of leading citizens petitioned the government, as they were "by the present laws ... deprived of the benefits of Public Registers to record the Births, Marriages and Deaths which occur among them by reason whereof ... are they exposed to serious inconvenience and loss."[30] An informal solution, commonly adopted by Jews who had no such registers, was to register the facts themselves in a family Hebrew prayer-book. George and Isabella Benjamin's children were not baptized at birth. The only record of the birth of each of them was an entry in a Hebrew prayer-book signed by their father, far away from any community of Jews. A third child, George Lipman, named after both George and his father-in-law, was born on 2 April 1837. Like his older brother and sister, his birth was entered in George Benjamin's prayer-book. Hannah Matilda Benjamin, born 2 May 1839, and Lewis Benjamin, born 9 November 1841, were both registered by George

Benjamin in his prayer-book.

If Benjamin had been comfortable before with the Christian prayers of an Orangeman, by the end of the decade he showed even more outward signs that he was assimilating into Christian society. The comment was made in town that Benjamin "passes here for a Christian, for he visits our church about once a year, and eschews all connexion with the Children of Israel." The observer, no friend of Benjamin's, could not let the moment pass without adding: "But he is a Jew by birth, and one at heart and in practice, and belongs to the very worst tribe of them."[31]

NOTES

[1] *Consolidated by laws for the City of Belleville* (1898), p. 12: "Members of the Board of Police and other officials of the Corporation of Belleville from 1836 to 1850." Benjamin's appointment took effect as of 1 January 1837. He was reappointed to the position every year until 1848.

[2] *British Whig*, 11 May 1838, p. 3, col. 2.

[3] "The Militia Register of Upper Canada with a Statement of the Volunteer Corps within the Province, and Dates of Commission, &c. &c. &c.," p. 25, bound in *Toronto Almanac* (Toronto, Palladium Office, 1839).

[4] *Ibid.*, p. 23. *See also* [Mackenzie Bowell], "George Benjamin, Esq." *Intelligencer*, 9 September 1864.

[5] Billa Flint to Sir George Arthur, March 1838. Colin Read and Ronald J. Stagg, *The rebellion of 1837* (Toronto, Champlain Society, 1985), pp. 376-77.

[6] *British Whig*, 11 May 1838, p. 3, col. 2. Barker, the editor, had come through difficult times. A reformer in politics until the rebellion, his paper was boycotted, his press was wrecked, and he was physically assaulted: J. W. Spurr, "Edward John Barker," *Dictionary of Canadian Biography*, vol. XI. His change in political philosophy to conservative in 1838 did not diminish his antagonism towards Benjamin.

[7] Henry Strauss Quixano Henriques, *Jews and the English law* (Oxford, 1908), reprinted from a series of 11 articles published between 1901 and 1907 in the *Jewish Quarterly Review. See* in particular "The civil rights of English Jews," 18 (1906), pp. 40-83. *See also* Arthur Brodey, "Political and Civil Status of the Jews of Canada,"

MA thesis, Jewish Institute of Religion, Cincinnati, Ohio, 1933, in the American Jewish Archives, Cincinnati.

8 "An Act for Naturalising such Foreign Protestants and Others therein mentioned, as are Settled or shall Settle in any of His Majesty's Colonies in America," 13 George II, c. 7 (1740), known as the Plantations Act. Section 4 permitted naturalization after seven years residence in the colonies. By section 3, Jews were allowed to amend the oath of abjuration in swearing loyalty to the crown by deleting the words "on the true faith of a Christian" from the text.

9 S. W. Rosendale, "An early ownership of real estate in Albany New York by a Jewish trader," *PAJHS*, vol. 3 (1895), pp. 61-71.

10 Lot A1, Collier's Division, Halifax Allotment, was granted to John Franks, Will Culbert, and Robert Barnstable: Halifax Allotment, Book 1, page 1, Provincial Crown Records Centre, Halifax, Nova Scotia.

11 In 1797 petitions by four Jews for grants of crown land in Upper Canada had been refused or postponed in deference to the view of the chairman of the Land Board, Chief Justice John Elmsley, who had recently arrived from England and who believed that "Jews cannot hold land in this Province." Other land officials ignored Elmsley's decision and completed one of the grants within two years. Finally, on 10 May 1803, in answer to the "Prayer for Relief" of Moses David of Sandwich (Windsor), the Executive Council formally decided that his religion did not "preclude him from any grant in His Majesty's Colonies," a decision that was confirmed by the lieutenant governor. A full account of the incident will appear in a subsequent work by the authors.

12 In 1830, for example, Samuel Becancour Hart, in a petition to the government of the Province of Lower Canada, confirmed that "The right of holding lands has never been disputed in this Prov^{ce} to persons of the Jewish faith." NAC, RG4, A-1, vol. 351 (1831), pp. 96-98.

13 Myer Michaels (1760-1815), a Jewish fur trader, received a crown grant from Lieutenant Governor Patrick Sinclair for a lot at Fort Michilimackinac at the strait where Lake Huron joins with lakes Michigan and Superior. *See* "Register of the Post of Michilimackinac, 1 June, 1785-[1787]" James Gruet, notary, p. 13 (in the possession of the clerk, Mackinac County Court House, St Ignace, Michigan). Mackinac Island, on which the fort is located, was part of Upper Canada until ceded by the British under Jay's Treaty in 1796.

14 Myer Solomons, a Jew, was approved for a crown grant of the east half of lot 25, concession 2 in the Cornwall area in 1789: PAO, Upper Canada Land Book, RG1, series A IV, vol. 8, p. 54. After locating on his land for a time, he sold his rights and returned to Montreal: item B1046, "Report of Claims Upon Land in the Eastern District decided by Hon W. D. Powell & his fellow Commissioners 24-29 August, 1799," manuscript records of D. W. Smith, surveyor general of Up-

per Canada, Baldwin Room, Metropolitan Toronto Library. John Lawe and John Levy Jacobs, both of Jewish descent and, at least in the case of Lawe, perceived as Jewish, received approval for town lots in Newark (now Niagara), Upper Canada, in 1794. *See* PAO, Upper Canada Land Petitions, "L" bundle misc. 1788-1795, and Upper Canada Land Petitions, "I-J" bundle misc. 1788-1795, respectively.

[15] Moses David was born in Montreal in 1767 and died in Sandwich, Upper Canada, on 27 September 1814. As to his militia appointments, *see John Askin Papers*, vol. II, ed. Milo M. Quaife (Burton Historical Records, Detroit Public Library, Detroit, 1931), p. 645. *See also* Return of Essex County Militia at Sandwich, 12 December 1807 signed by Moses David, Captain, in John Askin papers, Burton Historical Collection, Detroit Public Library. An outline of other appointments of Jews in the military in this period will be dealt with in a subsequent work.

[16] On 24 February 1808 Francis Gore, the lieutenant governor, had granted a commission to Moses David to serve as coroner of the Western District, a semi-judicial position analogous to a county-court clerk in Lower Canada: NAC, RG68, liber D, p. 13.

[17] Its full title was illuminating. It was called "An Act to dispense with the necessity of taking certain Oaths and making certain Declarations in the cases therein mentioned; and also to render it unnecessary to receive the Sacrament of the Lord's Supper as a qualification for Offices or for other temporal purposes." 3 William IV, c. 12, passed 29 November 1832, royal assent 13 February 1833.

[18] *Canadian Jewish Archives*, ed. David Rome, vol. 16 (1980), p. 149, quoting the Montreal *Gazette*, 24 January 1831.

[19] "Anecdote of the late Mr. Benjamin," *Chronicle and News* (Kingston), 16 September 1864, p. 3.

[20] Correspondence respecting George Benjamin by D. J. Sutherland, grand secretary of the Loyal Orange Grand Lodge, Province of Ontario East, 5 April and 9 April 1934: Hastings County Historical Society Collection, item no. 2445, Belleville Public Library.

[21] *Rules and Regulations of the Orange Institution of British North America* (Belleville, Thomas Tomkins, Printer, 1830), p. 1 (copy of mfm at the National Library of Canada).

[22] Jacob Henry's speech was made in support of his right to take his seat in the North Carolina House of Commons in 1808. *See infra*, chapter VIII, pp. 80-81.

[23] *Robertson's landmarks of Toronto*, ed. J. Ross Robertson, vol. VI, chapter 32, "The Glorious Twelfth," pp. 137-87, at p. 169.

[24] *Ibid.*

25 *Ibid.*, p. 168.

26 *Ibid.*, p. 179.

27 *Rules and Regulations of the Orange Institution*, p. 16.

28 *Infra*, chapter VI.

29 Aaron Ezekiel Hart (1803-57). His application to become a barrister, advocate, attorney, proctor, and solicitor is in NAC, RG4, B 8, vol. 21, file 1823-1824. His original oath is in RG1, E 11, vol. 4, file 1820-1830. *See also* Denis Vaugeois, "Aaron Ezekiel Hart," *Dictionary of Canadian Biography*, vol. VIII.

30 "Petition of the Jews of Montreal ... ," 4 December 1828, *Journals of the House of Assembly of Lower Canada*, vol. 38, p. 84. Reprinted in *Canadian Jewish Archives*, vol. 1, no. 6 (Bureau of Social and Economic Research, Canadian Jewish Congress, Montreal, 1962), pp. 1-6.

31 Moodie, *op. cit.*, p. 482. The observation can be dated to this period, for at the time of Moodie's comment Benjamin was "not above forty years old."

CHAPTER V

Making It in the Bush[1]

❧

"The Jew Editor is a true picture drawn from life
which so closely resembles the original that it will be
recognized by all who ever knew him, or fell under his
lash, a man detested in his day and generation."

Susanna Moodie, Belleville, to Richard Bentley,
London, 30 January 1854

IN HIS HANDS BENJAMIN HELD A NUMBER OF SHEETS OF PAPER, FOLDED DOUBLE,
about the size of a piece of roofing slate. He could not yet be certain to what
extent their words, like a verbal cannonade, had wounded him. He had
been held up to ridicule, his character blasted. The diatribe called him "a
man whom all men hate" and referred to him as a "laughing rogue" who
"will cheat you if he can," who, "between jokes and blarney dexterously
applied, contrives most effectively to pick your pocket." He is "a living,
laughing impersonation of gratuitous mischief," "a sort of moral hyena,"
"a more spiteful, wicked, malignant devil never received a commission
from Satan to trouble the earth."

The first page of the paper had large printed words set over a line "THE
LITERARY GARLAND. November, 1843." Under the line were more
words, set slightly smaller, "RICHARD REDPATH. A Tale. By Mrs
Moodie." This was the third monthly episode in a four-part serial.

The author of the piece, Susanna Moodie, lived in Belleville with her
husband, John Wedderburn Dunbar Moodie.[2] Moodie and his wife,
both writers, had come to Canada from England in 1832. Born in 1803,
she married Moodie in 1831.[3] After a difficult time as settlers on the

frontier, in October 1839 Dunbar Moodie had been appointed sheriff of the newly created Victoria District as a result of a petition written by his wife to Lieutenant Governor Sir George Arthur. The Moodies took up residence in Belleville but, from the outset, "as outsiders thrust into the public spotlight as a result of Dunbar's much envied appointment, they found themselves precariously placed."[4] The Moodies saw Benjamin as the source of the problem.

Susanna Strickland Moodie, author of Roughing it in the bush *and other bestsellers of the day, attacked Benjamin through her story of "Richard Redpath."*

The two previous episodes of "Richard Redpath," published in September and October in the *Literary Garland* of Montreal as well as in the Toronto *Star*, had been non-threatening, almost humorous. According to the storyline, a man and his twin brother had been shipwrecked off Jamaica and left without resources. The man, Robert Redpath, learned

THE LITERARY GARLAND.

Vol. I.   NOVEMBER, 1843.   No. 11.

RICHARD REDPATH*.

A TALE.

BY MRS. MOODIE.

CHAPTER V.

—

Some account of brother Robert.

—

"What shall I do with this money, to turn it to the best advantage for myself, and that dear madcap who has obtained it for me, in a manner so extraordinary?" said Robert Redpath, as he sauntered from the slave market, and bent his steps he knew not whither, and gazed around him with an anxious, restless glance.

The old adage—"light come—light go," flashed across his mind; and not being of a very sanguine temperament, he came to the sudden conclusion, that the gold so miraculously obtained, could never be lucky. Now, Richard would have considered it an interposition of Divine Providence in his behalf, and merrily and cheerfully would have set to work, to make the most of his unexpected treasure. But Robert and Richard, although brothers, and fondly attached brothers too, for they were twins, and only children, who had never been separated more than a few days from their birth, were very different characters. Robert was shy and timid—proud and extremely sensitive; and ill fitted by this peculiar temperament to cope with the ills of life. He hated trouble—was not over industrious—had a tolerable conceit of himself, and, if the truth must be spoken, was very fond of money, of fine clothes, and of exciting the sympathy and admiration of others. Vanity is not always confined to the gay and dashing, who seem to demand the attention and respect of the crowd. It often dwells under the most quiet, and apparently the most unostentatious exterior; and operates the most forcibly upon minds which take the most pains to conceal it from the observation of others. Robert, with all his reserve, possessed far more of this univer-

sal failing, so common to our fallen nature, than his gay, happy brother; and the sudden and violent manner in which he resented any affront offered to his dignity, would have proved to every one versed in the study of mankind that he was a very vain man. His present abject appearance touched him more sensibly than even the loss of property. He fancied that every eye was upon him, while in reality few regarded the poor, shabby emigrant at all. He was pushed about rudely by the crowd, and more than one person had told him to stand out of the way. His pride was taught a useful lesson—one that he had never learned from experience before—that he owed the personal respect with which he had hitherto been treated, more to his outward appearance than he was at first willing to admit.

"Alas!" thought he, "is a man only valued by the cut and quality of his coat? Were I dressed genteelly, I should command the respect of these strangers. Well, then, as so much depends upon a coat, the first thing I buy must be a fashionable suit of clothes; and then, although I shall not be one half-penny the richer or better; yet my dress, giving the lie to the poverty of my means, will make me pass current among these heartless worldlings for more than I am really worth. Oh, the short-sightedness and folly of mankind! If my brother could but view the world with my eyes, it would soon tame down the gaiety of his volatile spirit."

With his mind full of these thoughts, and in no very enviable or amiable mood, he entered a store, and enquired of a thin, satirical-looking man, waiting behind the counter, "where he could procure a suit of ready made clothes?"

The man regarded him with a contemptuous grin; and, thinking that he was some drunken, dissipated fellow, who had lost his garments in a

* Continued from page 419.

New Series. Vol. 1, No. 11.   61

"*Richard Redpath*" by Mrs Moodie as it appeared in the
Literary Garland, *November 1843.*

of the flourishing slave trade on the island, and had decided to sell his brother Richard into slavery, then buy him back for a lower price, allowing them both to survive on the profit. The third episode turned ugly. Robert, now financially secure from having sold his brother, was looking for a tailor to help him dress according to his station. He had been referred to Benjamin Levi, who was not only the "Jew editor" of the Jamaica *Observer* ("a violent party paper, which most strenuously opposed the abolition of the slave trade"), but who sold clothes on the side.

The fictional Benjamin Levi was unmistakably patterned on Belleville's George Benjamin and possessed all of his physical features. He was "a short, fat man, with broad shoulders, a head and neck like a bull." Like Benjamin, he had an unusually large head with a "quantity of coarse, curling black hair, which gave to it a more determined air of obstinacy, while it set off the rich dark complexion, without shading, or in the least degree softening, its hardened and audacious expression," an expression "which made him an object of disgust and aversion." He showed a perpetual grin, "which though meant for a smile, was but an acquired contortion to hide the evil workings of the spirit within, and served to display a malicious looking set of strong, white teeth, which seemed as if they were formed to bite and worry his species."[5] It was a caricature Benjamin could not escape. And his office, the "long, low loft" up two flights of stairs from the "black, ugly, forbidding looking door,"[6] had been "immortalized."[7]

The origins of Susanna Moodie's hostility to the "Jew editor" had coincided with Benjamin's first active involvement in provincial politics. In April 1841, in the first election after the Act of Union had united Upper and Lower Canada, the tory candidate for Hastings County was Edmund Murney, who had represented the area for the previous four years.[8] His opponent, Robert Baldwin, the reform leader, lived in Toronto.[9] As permitted by the law at the time, Baldwin had run in two ridings, the Fourth Riding of York and Hastings, in order to ensure his election.

The election in Hastings was a bitter one. The Orangemen, recalling opposition they had received at the hands of Baldwin's father when he was in the assembly years earlier, set themselves as a block against the son.[10] Murney, who had married Baldwin's first cousin,[11] was defeated by only 36 votes. Baldwin was also successful in York and he was forced to resign one of the seats. He resigned York on 25 August 1841, allowing Louis-Hippolyte La Fontaine, his co-leader, to be acclaimed in a by-election there on 8 September.

Murney's supporters, led by Benjamin, accused the returning officer in the Hastings election, Sheriff Moodie, with "intimidation perjury and partiality." Indeed, his independence of action was questionable. Though socially conservative, the Moodies did not fit into the tory order of politics nor into the Orange order of social and fraternal organization in Belleville. After his election, Baldwin came into contact with the Moodies. A mutual affection sprang up between them and their families. Baldwin did not spend much time in Belleville, but they corresponded often and Moodie did not hesitate to offer Baldwin partisan reports from Hastings.[12]

Events took another turn on 16 September 1842, when the governor general invited Baldwin and La Fontaine, who together commanded the support of a majority of the votes in the Legislative Assembly, to join his Executive Council or cabinet. The invitation was significant for the future of the Canadian political system as it marked the first time that a governor general had agreed to accept the leadership of the elected house as his formal advisors, even though his personal political views may have differed with theirs. This was "responsible government," which Baldwin and La Fontaine had championed as reformers, and it meant that the governor's advisors were responsible to the majority of the elected assembly, who were responsible in turn to the public, their electors. The governor general's invitation was also significant for George Benjamin in Hastings County. According to the law at the time, because their appointments were made more than 30 days after a general election, both Baldwin and La Fontaine were obliged to resign their seats in the assembly and be re-elected in by-elections as a condition of accepting positions in the Executive Council.

The Hastings by-election, called for 17 October 1842, turned out to be a rematch between Baldwin and Murney. It was one of the stormiest elections known in Canada. This time both tories and reformers appeared at the poll in armed groups prepared for violence. Charges of intimidation flew on both sides. Sheriff Moodie, again returning officer, attempted to restore order by calling out the local militia as well as two companies of government troops. By the time the poll had closed, Murney was ahead by 49 votes, although less than half the eligible voters had dared to come to the poll. Moodie's request to the authorities for an extension in the time for voting had been refused.[13]

On the basis of Moodie's report, the by-election was subsequently declared void. According to the official record, "a collision took place between the two parties causing conditions to be unsafe to poll all the votes of the county within the time prescribed by law."[14] For over a year, Hastings had no official representation in parliament.[15] At the beginning of November 1843, Murney was once again returned to the assembly as member for Hastings after a quiet by-election campaign in which Baldwin was no longer a candidate. Meanwhile, the blame for the disorder at the election of October 1842 had fallen on Moodie. Murney's chief lieutenant in the by-election, as well as in Moodie's subsequent discomfiture, was none other than George Benjamin, editor of the *Intelligencer*. He had helped incite tory and Orange feelings against Baldwin before the election and against Moodie afterwards. Benjamin had made other enemies as well. The partisan squabbles surrounding the elections had left a legacy of bitterness among Belleville's leading reformers and followers of Baldwin, men such as Billa Flint, William Hutton, and John Ross.

Billa Flint Jr earned his living as a merchant and miller, and was a force to be reckoned with in Hastings County politics. He had been born in 1805 near Brockville and had come to Belleville about 1820. When Belleville became incorporated as a police village in 1836, Flint was first president of the board or mayor, and was re-elected in 1839. Although no one knew it at the time, he was to defeat Edmund Murney as member of the assembly to represent Hastings South at the next general election, in 1847.[16]

William Hutton, on the other hand, never ran for public office, although he was associated with most of the prominent reformers in the Victoria District. He was born near Dublin in 1801 into a Protestant family and came to Belleville as a farmer in 1834. In 1841 he was appointed warden of Hastings County. He held the position until 1846, when an amendment to the Municipal Act made the position an elected one, and he decided not to run because, as he wrote to his mother, "there was no salary attached to it."[17] In 1843 he became superintendent of schools for the Victoria District. When it seemed as if the position of registrar of Hastings County would become vacant in 1844, in the words of John Ross, Baldwin's loyal aide and advisor, "Hutton applied as he does for every office that becomes vacant."[18]

It was John Ross who, as a young Belleville lawyer, persuaded Baldwin to run against Edmund Murney in Hastings County in 1841. He remained Baldwin's chief lieutenant in the area — the counterpart of George Benjamin's role in support of Edmund Murney — from that date until Baldwin arranged his appointment to the Legislative Council or "Upper Chamber" of the parliament of the Province of Canada in December 1848. Even though he spent most of his time out of Belleville after his appointment, he had numerous contacts with Benjamin in subsequent years.[19]

Benjamin had made enemies, but he had made many more friends. By his efforts, he had obtained great power and influence — a condition that produces enemies at the same time.[20] His enormous energy, his ability, and his cutting sense of humour had gained him the respect of all. In the words of his detractor, Susanna Moodie, "I don't know what we should do without Benjamin Levi — he keeps us all alive."[21]

NOTES

[1] The title was inspired by Susanna Moodie's major literary effort, *Roughing it in the bush* (1852).

[2] See Carl Ballstadt *et al.*, *Susanna Moodie: letters of a life time* (Toronto, University of Toronto Press, 1985), pp. 84-85. Born into a remarkable literary family, Susanna Strickland had received notice as a writer even before her marriage to Dunbar Moodie. Four of her five sisters, including Agnes Strickland and Catherine Parr Traill, as well as her brother, Samuel Strickland, were noted authors. She was later to be remembered for major contributions to Canadian literature in addition to *Roughing it in the bush*: *Life in the clearings* (1853) and *Flora Lyndsay* (1854). *See* C. P. A. Ballstadt, "Susanna Strickland (Moodie)," *Dictionary of Canadian Biography*, vol. XI.

[3] For Dunbar Moodie, *see* C. P. A. Ballstadt, "John Wedderburn Dunbar Moodie," *Dictionary of Canadian Biography*, vol. IX.

[4] Ballstadt *et al.*, *op. cit.*, p. 82.

[5] Moodie, *op. cit.*, p. 484.

6 *Ibid.*, pp. 483-84.

7 The phrase was Mackenzie Bowell's. *See Intelligencer*, 26 December 1862, quoted in Ballstadt *et al.*, *op. cit.*, pp. 88-89.

8 Edmund Murney was born at Kingston on 11 November 1812. He practised law after his call to the bar in 1834, becoming Belleville's first clerk of the peace as well as crown attorney. He served in the Upper Canada assembly as member for Hastings, 1836-1840; as well as in the assembly of the Province of Canada, 1843-48, 1851-56. In 1856 he was elected to the Legislative Council, a seat he held until his death in Belleville on 15 August 1861. *See* Dictionary of Canadian Biography (Toronto), biographical files; obituary in the *Globe* (Toronto), 17 August 1861; *Journal of Education for Upper Canada*, XIV (1861), p. 142.

9 Robert Baldwin (1808-58), the eldest son of Dr William Warren Baldwin, was born in York and called to the bar in 1825. In 1829 he was elected to the assembly for the Town of York but was defeated by W. B. Jarvis in 1830. In 1836 he was appointed to the Executive Council but resigned after four weeks, taking the rest of the council with him and precipitating a constitutional crisis in order to introduce his concept of responsible government. He was solicitor general (1840-41) and with Louis-H. La Fontaine formed ministries in 1842-43 and 1848-51.

10 In 1851 William Lyon Mackenzie, now the pardoned leader of the 1837 rebellion, told the parliament of the Province of Canada that, "when he first stood for the representation of Toronto against the Hon. Mr. Baldwin he was supported by all the Orangemen, and he could not understand why, until he had learned that the hon. gentleman's father had, whilst in Parliament, brought forward a bill to put them down." *Landmarks of Toronto*, vol. VI, John Ross Robertson, ed. (Toronto, J. Ross Robertson, 1914), p. 143.

11 Edmund Murney had married Maria Breakenridge, daughter of John Breakenridge and Mary Warren — William Warren Baldwin's sister. *See* R. M. and J. Baldwin, *The Baldwins and the great experiment* (Toronto, Longmans, 1969), pp. 169-70.

12 Boyce, *Historic Hastings*, pp. 46-97.

13 Ballstadt *et al.*, *op. cit.*, pp. 86-87.

14 *Legislators and legislatures of Ontario*, comp. and ed. Debra Forman (Ontario Legislative Library, Research & Information Series, 1984), vol. I, 1794-1866, p. 4.

15 One of Baldwin's supporters resigned his seat in Rimouski, and after being re-elected there, Baldwin resumed his place in the assembly before the end of January 1843.

16 Billa Flint Jr (1805-94) served as member of parliament for Hastings 1847-51, reeve of Belleville 1853-54, member of parliament for Hastings South 1854-57, reeve of Elzevir Township 1859-62, legislative councillor of Trent division 1863-67, mayor

of Belleville 1866, senator 1867-94. See Mika, *op. cit.*, pp. 3, 31, 194; *Legislators and Legislatures of Ontario*, vol. I (1792-1866), comp. and ed. Debra Forman (Toronto, Province of Ontario, Legislative Library, 1984); Larry Turner, "Billa Flint," *Dictionary of Canadian Biography*, vol. XII. Mackenzie Bowell described him as a Baldwin Reformer before 1867 and a supporter of Sir John A. Macdonald's Liberal-Conservative coalition after: *Debates of the Senate*, 15 June 1894, p. 563. As he was neither Liberal nor Conservative after 1867, the Kingston *British Whig* described him as a "loose fish" (1, 9 January 1898).

[17] Gerald E. Boyce, *Hutton of Hastings* (Belleville, Hastings County Council, *Intelligencer*, 1972), p. 136. *See also* Wesley B. Turner, "William Hutton," *Dictionary of Canadian Biography*, vol. IX.

[18] According to Belleville lawyer John Ross in a letter to Robert Baldwin, 8 May 1844, Boyce, *Hutton of Hastings*, p. 117. *See also* Paul Cornell, "John Ross," *Dictionary of Canadian Biography*, vol. X.

[19] Cornell, *loc. cit.* Ross (1818-71) married Baldwin's youngest daughter, Eliza, on 4 February 1851. He subsequently held a number of cabinet posts in the administrations led by Francis Hincks and Allan Napier McNab, as well as serving as speaker of the Legislative Council. After Hincks withdrew from politics in the summer of 1854, Ross actually became the leader of the moderate Reformers for a time before drifting over to support John A. Macdonald and his Conservatives by 1856.

[20] Moodie, *op. cit.*, p. 482.

[21] *Ibid.*, p. 560.

CHAPTER VI

Picking Up the Pieces

ॐ

"The Masters and officers of the
Grand Lodge having ineffectually endeavored to
get up petitions for the repeal of the Party Processions Act, he,
as the Grand Master, got up petitions which were presented
by Hon. John Ross in the Legislative Council and by
J. A. Macdonald in the House of Assembly."

Notes from an address by George Benjamin,
Grand Master of British North America, to a meeting of the
Toronto District Orange Lodge, 27 June 1851[1]

ON 26 NOVEMBER 1843, TWO WEEKS AFTER EDMUND MURNEY HAD BEEN RE-
elected to represent Hastings in parliament, the Baldwin-La Fontaine
ministry resigned. A tory government headed by William Henry Draper
and D. B. Viger was then appointed and held office by a narrow majority
until July 1847. Notwithstanding the impact of Susanna Moodie's
"Richard Redpath" in Belleville, the tory order had been re-established in
Hastings County and in the Province of Canada. In January 1844, only
a month after the last of the four episodes of "Richard Redpath" had been
published, George Benjamin was once again appointed clerk of the
Belleville Board of Police or town council. Of course there was the chance
he would be perceived as a "Jew Editor" in the words of Susanna Moodie
— a perception Benjamin set about to change.

Susanna Moodie had said that Benjamin "eschews all connexion with
the children of Israel." Indeed, it seems that he had only minimal contact
with other Jews from the time of his coming to Canada, primarily in
connection with the construction of the synagogue in Montreal in the mid

1830s. There were a number of Jewish families who settled in Toronto during the 1840s and who had established a communal cemetery by 1849. But there is no evidence that Benjamin had joined them even though Toronto was just over 100 miles away. Living in Belleville, a Christian community, Benjamin's Judaism had been a secular adherence on his part. He had also lost contact with his family in England.

The Benjamin family continued to grow. On 6 July 1844 a son, Ellis Ralph, was born. Another son, Harry Ansel, was born on 9 December 1845. Both births were recorded privately by George Benjamin in his small Hebrew prayer-book. Then, on 28 June 1846, George and Isabella Benjamin presented six-month-old Harry Ansel for public baptism at St Thomas' Church (Anglican) in Belleville by John Grier, rector.[2]

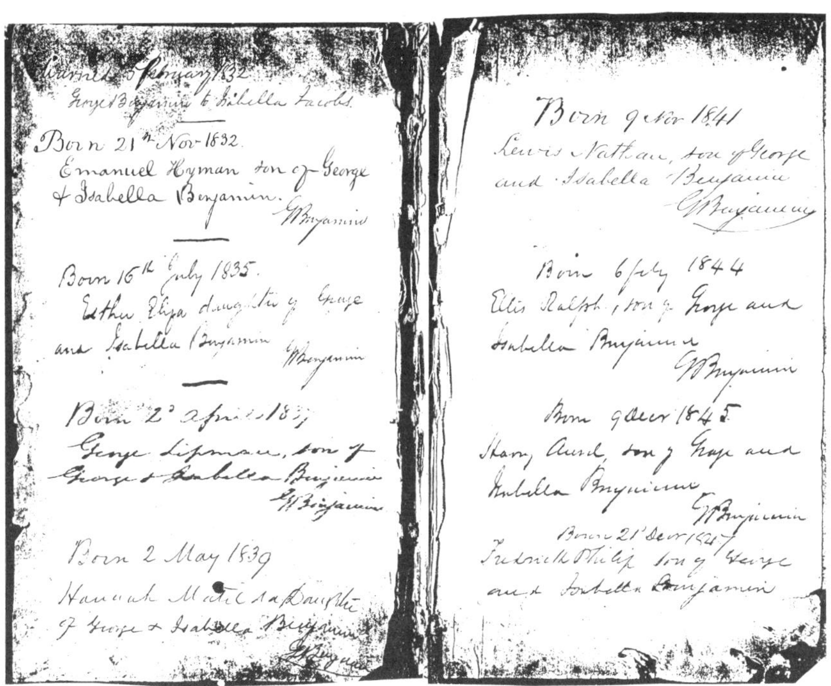

*Benjamin recorded his children's births on the front
and back covers of his Hebrew prayer-book.*

George Benjamin underwent a career change. By 1848 he had resigned as editor and publisher of the *Intelligencer*.[3] His replacement was his protégé, Mackenzie Bowell, now 25 years old, who, according to the evidence, had bought the paper along with his brother-in-law Rodney Moore, the printer. Benjamin's position as a public figure had grown with the *Intelligencer*'s circulation. But now it was time to distance himself from the intense personal exposure that had come from being associated with the paper as its publisher and editor. Although Benjamin's opponents continued to refer to Bowell as his "mercenary tool," Benjamin no longer appeared to be the owner of the paper.[4] In public perception, therefore, by 1848 Benjamin should no longer have been considered a Jew or an editor.

Mackenzie Bowell, c. 1848.

Meanwhile, he was continuing to pick up the pieces of a career that would lead him to higher office. In 1844 the Bank of Montreal had decided to open an office in Belleville, as the town had no bank. The bank was not yet ready to open a branch, but it wanted an agent, a capable, trustworthy administrator to help them establish a presence in town. Benjamin agreed to act as agent and opened an office in a one-room, red-brick building on the north side of Hotel Street, a short distance from the corner of Front Street.[5]

There is little doubt that Benjamin, who appeared to be a man devoted to his career, was also being driven by a larger objective. He had settled in a developing area that had no entrenched social establishment. He had been accepted freely as an equal, although the freedom he experienced may well have been due to the force of his personality. If Benjamin's children were to enjoy the same unrestricted opportunity as their father — George and Isabella had already brought six into the world by 1844 — the district had to develop and mature, and continue to ensure equality to those of a different background. Benjamin chose to work for the provision of a public infrastructure: good schools; good transportation in the form of roads, bridges and even rail lines; a good business environment; and finally, good government. His larger objective obliged him to move into as many fields as possible. Benjamin's appointment in February 1844 as Belleville's first superintendent of common schools was in keeping with his objective.[6] As one of the most literate people in the district, he started on a ten-year project to reorganize the common or public schools by consolidating small schools into districts, instituting a prize system for students and assisting poor sections.[7]

At the same time, Benjamin continued to participate in other efforts to help the district develop. In 1846 he became secretary of the newly incorporated Wolfe Island, Kingston, and Toronto Railroad, which hoped to bring the rail line to Belleville. He thus became the first Jew on record as a shareholder of a corporation in Canada West.

Then, that same year, a major appointment came his way as the result of a scandal involving the land registrar of Hastings County, Allan McLean. A lawyer with a long career of some distinction, a founder of the Law Society of Upper Canada, and a member of the House of Assembly for 17 years, including 8 as speaker, McLean had been registrar for almost 50 years. In 1833, when he was over 80, he had his son, Robert Charles Archibald McLean, appointed deputy registrar, hoping that his son would carry out the functions of the office while he remained nominally responsible. By 1846, when he was 94, almost 3,000 documents, for which the registrar had been duly paid, had been left unregistered.[8]

This was a scandal. According to the Registry Act, the purpose of registering titles to land was to give notice to the public of ownership as well as changes in ownership. If land transfers were not registered when they were supposed to be, then the public would be entitled to assume that some former owner, who had in fact sold his land and been paid for it, was still the owner. In May 1846 Victoria District Council petitioned the governor general to have McLean removed. Instead, he resigned. But after his resignation was accepted, it was withdrawn. In the resulting turmoil, the district council again petitioned the government, citing McLean's "long and disgraceful delinquency" and asking "that Your Excellency will be pleased to appoint a capable person, *not a lawyer*, to the office of the Registrar for the county at as early a period as possible."[9] The government refused to allow McLean to withdraw his resignation and, in response to the public outcry, the assembly on 18 May 1846 passed an "Act to remedy defects in the Registration of Titles in the County of Hastings in Upper Canada."[10] In view of the obvious lack of adequate standards of conduct for registrars, later in the year the government passed an amendment to the Registry Act to provide, by section 21, that in the future, if any registrar or his deputy should neglect his duty as set out in the act, the registrar would forfeit his office.[11]

On 8 August 1846 the government led by William Henry Draper appointed George Benjamin registrar of Hastings County, to clean up the mess.[12] He had been appointed over William Hutton, warden of Victoria District and an able administrator.[13] Whether or not the appointment[14] was for "his services to his party," as Mackenzie Bowell later suggested, or because of his undoubted abilities, the appointment was a vote of confidence in Benjamin.

The registrarship was an enormous job. The salary was dependent upon the volume of business done by the registry office, and in view of the huge backlog, a generous salary was guaranteed. Life had changed for Benjamin. He now had a government appointment and a dependable income. He could start thinking about how else to serve his community.

Before the end of 1846 Benjamin was elected grand master of the

Orange order of British North America, an organization 50,000 strong.[15] Though it was perceived to be a Protestant organization (indeed its by-laws in the 1870s allowed only Protestant members), no one in the organization felt there was a necessity for excluding other non-Catholic members in its formative period. Benjamin's election represented a renewed consolidation of conservative and Orange interests, a unity that had been threatened when his predecessor as grand master, Ogle Robert Gowan of Brockville, had antagonized tories by denouncing the ruling oligarchy, the "family compact." More than that, his election represented a remarkable personal achievement: Benjamin had become the leader of what was probably the largest and best organized political lobby group in the province.

Benjamin held the position for seven years. It was a period highlighted by the Orange order's participation in the attacks on Governor General Lord Elgin for acceding to the decision of the majority in the assembly and signing the Rebellion Losses Bill which allowed for compensation of the families of the rebels in the 1837 rebellion. It was a period that included the burning of the Parliament Buildings in Montreal by an angry mob protesting against Lord Elgin's surrender to "Responsible Government" in 1849. In 1851 Benjamin helped secure the repeal of the legislation banning Orange processions, legislation that had been passed after the Hastings by-election nine years earlier by the ministry led by Robert Baldwin.[16] By 1853 Gowan had succeeded in reasserting his leadership, and at the Grand Lodge meeting in Kingston that year, the order split into two, with Gowan leading the majority of the lodges and Benjamin leading a large group that had withdrawn to form a schismatic Grand Lodge. In 1856 both grand masters resigned, ending the schism in the Orange order, which was reunited under a new, neutral leader.

There were other changes in the Benjamins' personal lives. In November 1846 Benjamin completed his purchase of a one-acre lot on the south side of the Dundas Highway.[17] It was a choice property on the escarpment, with an unobstructed view of the Bay of Quinte to the south. He was building a large two-storey brick mansion to accommodate a growing household. According to family records, Isabella Benjamin's father, Lipman Jacobs, had died in New Orleans. Isabella invited her mother, Esther, and a brother, Jacques, to come up to Belleville and live with her. She must have been pleased when they agreed. She would be reunited with her family.[18]

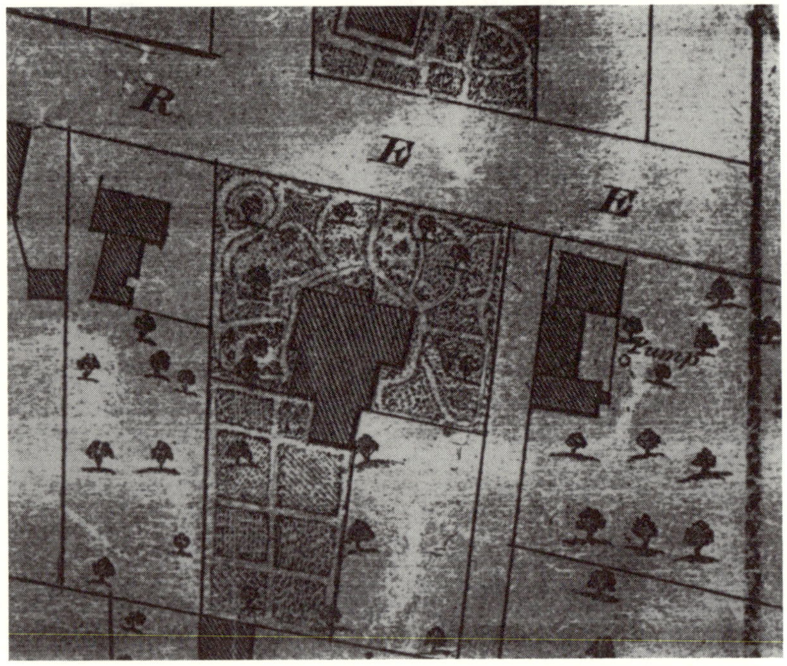

Plan of the Benjamins' 22-room mansion situated on the south side of the Dundas Highway opposite William Street, c. 1849.

NOTES

[1] From a newspaper account of Benjamin's speech, Robertson's *Landmarks*, VI, p. 145.

[2] St Thomas' Church records, Belleville, register no. 7-B-3, p. 253. The registers are in the custody of the Incorporated Synod of the Diocese of Ontario, Kingston. This

was not the pattern Benjamin followed with the other children, so it is possible to speculate that Harry Ansel might have been sickly and was baptized in order to be buried locally if necessary.

3   Nick and Helen Mika, *Mosaic of Belleville* (Belleville, Mika Silk Screening Limited, 1966), p. 169. The authors state that Bowell became editor and publisher in 1848 and sole proprietor in 1851. No source for this information is given. *See also* William H. Cooper "Introduction" to mfm of Belleville newspapers, PAO accession no. 6806.

4   "J. F." in the *Hastings Chronicle* (Belleville), 7 August 1861, says in part: "Why should we hold Mr. Benjamin responsible for the Articles in the Intelligencer? It is well known that it is his mouthpiece, but that it always attempts to excuse all the acts of corruption and mal-administration of which he has been guilty, ... that he is the editor in chief of that journal." There may have been something to the *Hastings Chronicle's* suspicion that Bowell was owner in name only. As Benjamin's daughter, Hannah ("Tilly") Macdonald (1839-1925), recalled at the age of 87, Bowell did not actually become the owner until after 1864. She recalled that after her father died, Bowell then "managed the paper for Mrs. Benjamin. Later a company was formed and Mackenzie Bowell became the chief stockholder." *See* "The birth of a paper," *Intelligencer*, 14 June 1924.

5   Bank of Montreal Archives, Montreal. *See also* Mika, *Mosaic of Belleville*, p. 83. Benjamin's involvement in banking was not unprecedented or unusual, notwithstanding his Jewish background. David David (1764-1824) had been one of the founding directors of the Bank of Montreal in 1818. Moses Hart (1768-1852) had operated Hart's Bank as a private bank in Three Rivers, Lower Canada, from 1835 (after his application for a chartered bank had been refused) until about 1847; it actually issued scrip in 1837 and 1838. Henry Hague Judah (1808-83) was one of the founding directors of the Montreal City and District Savings Bank in 1846 and served as its president from 1873 to 1877, although his mother was not Jewish, and he may have been baptized at his birth. Abraham Joseph (1815-86) was president of the Stadacona Bank from the time it was chartered in Quebec in 1872 until it went into voluntary liquidation in 1879.

6   Village of Belleville, Board of Police, *Minutes*, vol. 1, p. 103, 24 February 1844 (in the possession of the Belleville City Council). Common schools were the elementary schools of the day, open to all, although a small fee was usually charged in Belleville schools prior to 1850. The superintendent was required to supervise the schools — about four in number in 1844 — examine teachers, distribute the small annual government grants, and submit annual reports to the Education Office in Toronto. The authors are indebted to Gerald E. Boyce of Belleville, historian and author, for the information contained in notes 6 and 7.

7   *Ibid.*, p. 105, 20 March 1844. Benjamin continued his interest in education in later years. In 1850 and 1851 he introduced reforms into the school system as superintendent of schools for Hungerford Township: PAO, RG2, series C-6-C, vol. 8, no. 211, 5 February 1850; Annual Report from George Benjamin, Esq., as Hungerford

Township School Superintendent in *Canada Legislative Assembly, Journals, 1852-53*, app. JJ. Further reforms of the school system were introduced by Benjamin as chairman of the Belleville Board of School Trustees in 1854 and 1855: Minutes of the Belleville Board of Education, PAO, RG2, series F-3-E, 12, 19, and 26 January 1854, 27 January 1855, and 18 January 1856.

8 Lieut. Col. Allan Neil McLean (MacLean) was born in Scotland in 1752 and died near Kingston in 1847. His son Robert Charles Archibald McLean (1806-46), a bachelor, was deputy registrar from 19 January 1833 to 4 October 1844. He became mayor of Kingston in 1846. Smith continued the practice of his predecessor by receiving payment for and executing instruments tendered to him for registration, without registering them. Stearne Tighe MacLean, *Biography of Allan Neil MacLean of Kingston* (1967), bound typescript in Kingston; *Dictionary of Canadian Biography*, unpublished notes; obituary in *Globe*, 13 October 1847; W. R. Riddell, *The legal profession in Upper Canada* (1916), pp. 161-65, Graeme Patterson, "Allan McLean," PhD. thesis, University of Toronto, 1968.

9 "Journal — Victoria District, 1842-1846," being Victoria District *Records and Proceedings*, vol. I, pp. 185-87 [15 May 1846]; 208-214 [12 November 1845], in possession of the clerk, County of Hastings, Belleville.

10 9 Victoria, c. 12 (18 May 1846). The act referred to the neglect of Robert C. A. McLean as deputy registrar, in failing to register title documents such as deeds and mortgages that he had certified were registered. The act recited that "great injury and loss may arise from such neglect" because of those who might have dealt with the land without knowledge of unregistered instruments. As a remedy, the act allowed holders of title documents signed by Robert C. A. McLean but not registered, to be brought into the new registrar for retroactive registration at any time prior to 31 December 1846. The following year it was discovered that the situation was more long standing than it had first appeared. Robert Smith, who had also served as a deputy registrar under Allan McLean, from 1821 to 1844, had apparently followed the same practice. As a result, a new act was passed, 10-11 Victoria, c. 38 (9 July 1847), to allow the late registration of instruments signed by Robert Smith, but not registered, in the same manner as those signed by Robert McLean, but not registered. The deadline for late registration was extended to 31 December 1847.

11 9 Victoria, c. 34 (1846).

12 *Canada Gazette*, 1846, p. 3044.

13 Boyce, *Hutton of Hastings*, p. 117.

14 [Mackenzie Bowell], "George Benjamin, Esq.," *loc. cit.*

15 Hereward Senior, "George Benjamin," *Dictionary of Canadian Biography*, vol. IX. *See also* Ballstadt *et al.*, *op. cit.*, p. 82.

16 It is a considerable irony that years later, Toronto's first Jewish mayor, Nathan Phillips, effectively ended the Orange procession in Toronto by refusing to lead

the parade on the "glorious twelfth" of July, a practice that previous mayors had all followed.

17 Deed from James Ketcham to George Benjamin, part of south half of lot 5, con. 1, Thurlow Township, registered 30 November 1846 as no. R.353 in Hastings County Registry Office, Belleville. The foundation of the house is shown on a "Plan of the Town of Belleville, County of Hastings and District of Victoria by John J. Haslett, D. P. Surv^r." on file in the Department of Survey Records, Ontario Ministry of Natural Resources, Toronto as no. R14-4. The authors are indebted to Gerald E. Boyce for the information that the plan was prepared by October 1845.

18 "George Benjamin File," notes by Rosetta Benjamin Gemmell Shaw (1858-1949), daughter of George and Isabella Benjamin, donated to the Belleville Public Library, Hastings County Historical Society Collection, item no. 2385. The relevant note is as follows: "Mother (Isabella Jacobs) was born in New Orleans 1819. Her Parents were Dutch, born in Holland; One brother Jaques. My grandmother on Mother's side was a Heine. When her husband died, she came to Mother's to live; her brother visited her and then returned supposedly to Amsterdam; never heard of after."

"Benjamin's House" sketched by John D. Evans, architect,
Belleville, 19 March 1872.

George Benjamin, oil painting by William Sawyer, 1847.

Isabella Benjamin, oil painting by William Sawyer, 1847.

CHAPTER VII

The Politician

è&

> "I A.B. do ... solemnly and sincerely declare, that I do
> believe in my conscience, that not any of the descendants
> of the person who pretended to be Prince of Wales during the
> life of the late King James the Second ... hath any right, or title
> whatsoever, to the Crown of this realm or any other the domin-
> ions thereunto belonging ... . And I do make this recognition,
> acknowledgement, abjuration, renunciation and promise,
> heartily, willingly, and truly upon the true faith of
> a CHRISTIAN. – So help me GOD."

*The oath of abjuration in use in the Province of Upper Canada
from 9 July 1792 to 13 February 1833*

NOW IN HIS MID 40S, BENJAMIN HAD REACHED A TURNING POINT. HERE IN
Canada he had held positions of public trust of a kind that would have
been unheard of for a Jew a generation earlier. All of those had been
appointed positions, with the exception of his election as clerk of Thurlow
ten years before. Running for election to other, more responsible public
offices seemed to be a logical step forward.

At the beginning of 1847, Benjamin was once again appointed clerk
of Thurlow. But this time he was also interested in elected political office.
He ran for district councillor of Hungerford Township, north of
Belleville, and was elected. This position automatically gave him a seat on
Victoria District Council. Prior to this time the position of warden had
been an appointed one. Since an amendment to the Municipal Act had
made the position an elected one without a salary, William Hutton, the
previous warden, stepped aside and was content to be appointed clerk at

a salary of £40 a year.[1] At the first meeting of the newly elected district council, on 2 February 1847, George Benjamin was unanimously chosen as the first elected warden, making him the senior official in an area (including Belleville and the surrounding townships), responsible for roads, schools, public works, and other matters of common concern, including the land registry system for which, incidentally, Benjamin was still the registrar.

At the same time as Benjamin was appointed registrar of Hastings County, the Bank of Montreal was ready to open a branch in town in a new office with a full-time manager. Benjamin, who already had his time occupied, ended his role of agent for the bank.[2] He did find time, however, to be involved in the provincial election of December 1847. The reformers, led by Robert Baldwin in Canada West and Louis-H. La Fontaine in Canada East, made an extremely strong showing. In Hastings, to Benjamin's chagrin, Edmund Murney, the conservative incumbent, lost to Billa Flint, the former mayor of Belleville.

As always, the Benjamins demonstrated a continuing concern about their children and their future chances of success. That autumn, Emanuel Hyman (or "Mannie" as the family called him) was enrolled at Upper Canada College in Toronto[3] and Esther Eliza ("Ettie") was sent to boarding school in Montreal.[4] On Friday, 24 September 1847, after the Jewish high holy days, the Benjamins arranged the baptism at St Thomas' Church of their two oldest children, Mannie, born 1832, and Ettie, born 1836, just before the school season began.[5] Then, towards the end of the year, on 21 December 1847, the Benjamins had another child, their eighth. The birth of Frederick Philip was registered by George Benjamin in his Hebrew prayer-book. It was as if Benjamin had wanted to record for the future that deep inside he was still a Jew.

The Benjamins' new house was finished over the winter, even though the construction had cost much more than expected and the property had to be mortgaged to cover part of the cost of the bills.[6] In the summer, tragedy overtook the Benjamins when their third child, 11-year-old George Lipman, drowned. He had not been baptized and could not be buried in the cemetery of St Thomas' Church. Probably to lessen the possibility of this situation recurring, on 12 September 1848 the

Benjamins had three more of their children baptized: Hannah Matilda Jane, Lewis Nathan, and Ellis Ralph.[7] After that time there were no more entries in the small, leather-bound Hebrew prayer-book.

The following year, 1848, Benjamin gave up his position as clerk of Thurlow. He was re-elected as a district councillor and unanimously won re-election as warden. William Hutton, who as Benjamin's predecessor in the position of warden had been no friend to Benjamin, found that his position as clerk was not renewed by the new council.

William Hutton (1801-61).
Hutton "applied for every office that came available."
He was no friend of Benjamin's.

In 1849 Benjamin was easily re-elected as warden, although it was to be his last year in that office. The district was being reorganized as the County of Hastings under the Municipal Act of 1849. This act converted all districts throughout the province into counties, provided for the incorporation of villages and towns, and increased the powers of local, municipal government.[8] At the beginning of the year, a scandal broke out, with unfortunate implications for Benjamin. It involved the previous district treasurer, Phillip Ham. In 1847 the district council had authorized the treasurer to receive contributions for "the relief of the destitute and suffering" in the Irish potato famine. A year or so later, when Ham died, it was found that some of the contributions were missing. What was worse, George Benjamin had served formally as his assistant. William Hutton, still stinging from council's failure to reappoint him as clerk a few months earlier, publicly accused him of complicity in the treasurer's default, in a manner that neutral parties regarded as libellous.[9] The issue finally came to the district council, where by a vote of nine to three it was decided that the charges against Benjamin were "without fact or foundation." Mrs Ham, the treasurer's widow, offered to replace the missing money in any event.[10]

By the end of 1849, Benjamin had presided over the growth of the district for three years. "It was he," Mackenzie Bowell recalled later, "who first endeavoured to induce our people to build the plank road from Belleville to Canifton [*sic*], failing in this he persuaded an American to undertake the task, which proved to be the best paying stock in Canada."[11] Benjamin's own account of the plank road achievement had been no less glowing. "I do but justice to the Contractors," he said, "when I say that it is generally regarded as one of the best, if not the very best[,] Roads of the Kind, ever built."[12] When the year was over, he received the thanks of district council, which, at the end of its term, in October 1849, presented Benjamin with "an elegant silver mug, with an inscription engraved thereon, expressive of their high appreciation of his services to the County."[13]

In January 1850 Benjamin was again elected to the council of Hungerford Township and selected as its reeve. When he went to the first meeting of the County of Hastings Council, at the beginning of February, he had every reason to expect to become its first warden. He was nominated, to run against Edward Fidlar of Rawdon Township, but when the vote was taken, Fidlar had the distinction of becoming first warden, by a vote of seven to four over Benjamin.[14] Six of Fidlar's seven votes came from the prosperous area in the south of the county — the townships of

The *"elegant silver mug"* *"presented to George Benjamin, Esq.*
by the Municipal Council of the District of Victoria as a
Mark of the appreciation of his services as Warden of the
District of Belleville, October 1849."

Thurlow and Sidney and the newly incorporated town of Belleville. It was becoming increasingly obvious that George Benjamin's support was coming from the "underprivileged" townships in the north of the county, even though he himself lived in Belleville.

In the previous year's election for warden, the last in the old Victoria District, Benjamin had won over Joseph Caniff of Thurlow Township by a vote of ten to three.[15] Now, when the new county council met, only three of the fifteen councillors had been on the previous council. Belleville, as a police village, had not had independent representation. At the end of 1849, however, it had been incorporated as a town and now sent two representatives to council — Reeve Rufus Holden and Deputy Reeve Samuel Stevens — both of whom voted against Benjamin. At the same time Benjamin had lost support when the rural northern townships of Elzevir and Madoc had been combined at the end of 1849, leaving them with a total of two votes instead of four.[16]

Benjamin's loss of the position of warden to Edward Fidlar in 1850 was the first setback in his career. He was still reeve of Hungerford, but he had lost a position that he had counted on. In 1851, however, he was again elected reeve of Hungerford, and this time succeeded in becoming

Hastings County Court-House (meeting place
of the Hastings County Council) sat high on the hill
overlooking the city of Belleville.

warden of Hastings County, winning over Benjamin F. Davey, reeve of Belleville, by a vote of nine to six.[17] He remembered the lesson of his defeat the previous year and "undertook to advocate the cause of the rear Townships, and sought to place them on an equal footing with the front Townships," which included Belleville.[18] During his first year as warden tragedy again struck Benjamin's family with the death of his ninth child, Charles Angus, born just two years before. He was buried on 17 September in the cemetery of St Thomas' Church in Belleville.[19]

St Thomas' Church in Belleville, c. 1845,
showing the cemetery at left.

At the end of the year there was another provincial election, which the reformers lost heavily. Baldwin, whose government had resigned the previous August, lost his seat in York. And what was equally important, Benjamin's candidate, Edmund Murney, had succeeded in defeating Billa Flint in Hastings. A month later, when Benjamin again ran for warden, for the year 1852, he was unopposed.

Billa Flint Jr (1805-94).
Flint, a Reformer in politics,
opposed Benjamin at every turn.

Edmund Murney (1812-61).
Murney dominated Conservative politics
in Hastings County for the 20 years
before his election to the Legislative
Council in 1856.

At the municipal elections in 1853, Benjamin faced an unanticipated contest for the office of warden. Having lost his seat in parliament to Murney, Billa Flint had been elected reeve of Belleville and had decided to run against Benjamin for the warden's position. The town of Trenton had been incorporated during the previous year and therefore had one vote in addition to Sidney Township, from which it had been separated. When the vote was taken, each of the candidates had seven votes, with Trenton's reeve voting for Flint. The minutes of the meeting described what happened next: "The Township of Tyendinaga having more free holders and householders on the Collector's Roll for the preceding year, than any other municipality in the County of Hastings, the Reeve of said Township had therefore the casting vote." Reeve Nathaniel S. Appleby cast his vote in favour of Benjamin, thus re-electing him as warden — an act of support that Benjamin never forgot.[20] The following year, 1854,

Flint again ran against Benjamin but this time Benjamin triumphed, nine votes to five.[21]

George Benjamin could have been proud of his achievements. He had been the first Jew elected to any municipal office in Canada. Jews had been effectively excluded from office in municipal corporations in Lower Canada until the Declaratory Act of 1832[22] and in Upper Canada until the oath was amended in 1833.[23] In England it was even later that Jews were generally able to be elected as officers of municipal corporations. David Salomons was elected alderman for the City of London in 1847, only after the Jewish Disabilities Removal Act was passed in 1845.[24] There had been exceptions in the case of unincorporated municipalities, however, such as Benjamin's uncle Hyam Lewis, elected to the Brighthelmstone Board of Commissioners in 1822, and Phineas Levi, elected to the Devonport Board of Commissioners in 1830.

Benjamin had been elected clerk of Thurlow Township in 1836.[25] He had been honoured by the appointment as Belleville's first superintendent of common schools. He had been elected as councillor for Hungerford Township in January 1847 and, in the same year, had been elected warden for Victoria District, the highest municipal office in the area, holding the position until the end of 1849 when the district was reconstituted. In 1850 he had been elected reeve of Hungerford Township, the equivalent of its mayor.[26] He had again become warden of the area renamed the County of Hastings in 1851 and was subsequently reelected to the post each year.

But weaknesses in Benjamin's chosen way of life were beginning to assert themselves. His political defeat for the office of warden in 1850 had also been an economic set back. In March 1851 he borrowed £600 on a second mortgage against his house[27] from the Reverend George Romanes, who had just settled in Belleville after a term as professor of classical literature at Queen's College.[28] In 1850 Benjamin sorely missed the county warden's salary. It had been worth £100 a year, and if he had worked harder than expected, the council might have voted an additional honorarium.[29] He had ended his agency for the Bank of Montreal three years earlier, and he had sold his interest in the *Intelligencer*. Added to his other debts of maintaining his house, sending the children away to school, and supporting his growing family, Benjamin was under some pressure. The Benjamin family's financial pinch was a minor one, but the event had long-term significance: a politician who chooses to limit his sources of income to those of his office becomes more vulnerable as his dependence on his elected office increases. Benjamin was confronted by the eternal questions that have always faced professional politicians: "How will you support your family?" and "What will you do when the job finishes?"

NOTES

1 Boyce, *Hutton of Hastings*, pp. 404-5.

2 Bank of Montreal Archives, *loc. cit.*

3 *Roll of Pupils of Upper Canada College Toronto January 1830 to January 1916*, ed. A. H. Young (Kingston, Hanson, Crozier, and Edgar, 1917), p. 108. Emanuel Hyman Benjamin was first enrolled in 1847.

4 Ruby Milburn (a granddaughter of the Benjamins), "George Benjamin File," Hastings County Historical Society Collection, item. no. 2385, p. 3, Belleville Public Library. The date of her commencement at boarding school is not given but age 11 (in 1847) was possible.

5 St Thomas' Church records, *loc. cit.*, register no. 7-B-3, p. 293. The Jewish high holiday of Yom Kippur fell on Monday, 20 September 1847; the holy day of Succoth fell on Saturday, 25 September, commencing at sundown on the 24th.

6 Mortgage to cover a loan of £150 given by George Benjamin to George Filliter, 2 May 1848 and registered 13 May 1848 in the Registry Office for the County of Hastings as no. A161 for the Town of Belleville. The description of the lands provides in part, "and upon which said premises the said George Benjamin lately erected a brick dwelling house."

7 St Thomas' Church records, *loc. cit.*, register no. 7-B-3, p. 320. There is no record of the burial of George Lipman Benjamin in the registers.

8 The Municipal Act, 12 Victoria, c. 78 (1849), popularly known as the Baldwin Act.

9 Boyce, *Hutton of Hastings*, p. 168.

10 Boyce, *Historic Hastings*, p. 90.

11 [Mackenzie Bowell], "George Benjamin, Esq." *Intelligencer*, 9 September 1864. The *Intelligencer* for that date is not on microfilm, but copies are available from Hastings County Historical Society Collection, item no. 748, Belleville Public Library; *Kingston News*, 9 September 1864, p. 2; clipping in Isaac Buchanan Papers, NAC, MG24, 016, p. 1647.

12 George Benjamin, "Address" on retiring as warden for the Victoria District, appendix to meeting of the Victoria District Council, Wednesday, 30 October 1849, Victoria District/Hastings County *Records and Proceedings*, vol. II (1847-61) being the records of the proceedings of the Victoria District Council (January 1847 to December 1849) and the records of the Hastings County Council (January 1850 to February 1861), pp. 178-84, at p. 182, in the possession of the clerk, County of Hastings, Belleville.

13 [Bowell], "George Benjamin, Esq.," 9 September 1864. The "mug," a two handled ceremonial loving cup, is still in the possession of the Benjamin family.

14 Victoria District *Records and Proceedings*, vol. II, pp. 190-91.

15 *Ibid.*, pp. 119-20.

16 *Ibid.*, pp. 119-20, 186, 191-92. Hastings County had been consolidated into 12 townships and the Town of Belleville by 1851: 14 and 15 Victoria, c. 5, section 15.

17 Victoria District *Records and Proceedings*, vol. II, p. 253.

18 [Mackenzie Bowell], "George Benjamin, Esq.," *loc. cit.*

19 St Thomas' Church records, *loc. cit.*: birth 24 August 1849 and baptism 12 October 1849 (register no. 7-B-3, p. 360); death 16 September 1851 (register no. 7-B-3, p. 409).

20 Victoria District *Records and Proceedings*, vol. II, p. 507. Nathaniel Stephen Appleby was born in Prince Edward County in 1820 and died by 1891.

21 *Ibid.*, pp. 557-58.

22 1 William IV, c. 57 (Lower Canada, 1832).

23 3 William IV, c. 13 (Upper Canada, 1833).

24 8 & 9 Victoria, c. 52 (England, 1845). A similar measure had passed the House of Commons in 1841 but was rejected by the House of Lords 98 votes to 64. Salomons had been elected alderman for the City of London in 1835 and in 1844, although both times he was unable to subscribe to the declaration required and

was not admitted to office. The form of the declaration was as follows: "I, A.B., do solemnly and sincerely in the presence of God profess, testify, and declare, upon the true faith of a Christian, That I will never exercise any power, authority, or influence which I may possess by virtue of the office of ___________ to injure or weaken the Protestant Church as it is by law established in England, or to disturb the said Church or the said Bishops and Clergy of the said Church in the possession of any rights or privileges to which such Church or the said Bishops or Clergy are or may be by law entitled." *See* Henriques, "The Political Rights of English Jews," part 1, *loc. cit.*, at pp. 324-33.

[25] *Supra*, chapter IV, p. 33.

[26] Benjamin was followed as a municipal politician by Samuel C. Benjamin (*c.* 1813-93), of no apparent relation, who was elected to Montreal City Council in 1849. *See Star* (Montreal), 30 December 1893, "The Spanish and Portuguese Jews of Montreal." William Hyman (1807-82) was elected first mayor of the Township of Cape Rosier in the Gaspé for 1858 and for the next 24 years. A. D. Hart, *The Jew in Canada* (Toronto, 1926), p. 333. Lumley Franklin (1812-73) was elected mayor of Victoria for the year 1866. C. E. Leonoff, *Pioneers, pedlars and prayer shawls* (Victoria, B. C., Sono Nis Press, 1978), pp. 166-67.

[27] Mortgage, dated and registered 16 March 1850 as no. A202 for the City of Belleville, Hastings County Registry Office.

[28] George Romanes was educated in Edinburgh and ordained at Smith's Falls, Upper Canada, in 1834. After his stay in Belleville he returned to Edinburgh. He died in London on 18 February 1871. *See* Dictionary of Canadian Biography, notes; *Journal of Education for Ontario*, XXIV (1871), p. 29.

[29] As did the council in 1855, when it voted Benjamin £150, in addition to his regular payment of £100, for his "unusual services rendered during the year," Victoria District *Records and Proceedings*, vol. II, pp. 605 and 686.

CHAPTER VIII

Parliament

FOR SOME, CHANGES IN POSITION APPEAR AS A THREAT TO STABILITY. FOR OTHERS, such changes appear as a challenge. Early in 1854 an event occurred that tested George Benjamin's career as a politician as well as his ability to adapt to changing circumstances. Benjamin had been registrar of Hastings County for eight years, and had done an extraordinary job of re-establishing the registry system on an efficient basis. As Bowell recalled the event, "through an error on the part of a clerk in the office for which as Registrar he was responsible, he was dismissed by the Baldwin-La Fontaine Ministry more on an account of his political proclivities than from any wrong that he had done."[1]

What actually happened has been obscured by the passage of time, as the local newspapers of the day have been lost and the court records cannot be found. An order-in-council dated 1 May 1854 announced that the government had appointed "William Hamilton Ponton, of Belleville, Esquire, to be Register for the County of Hastings, in the place of George Benjamin, Esquire, who has forfeited the said Office."[2] Forfeit of the office did not mean that the registrar had resigned. The Registry Act in force at the time provided that "if any Registrar or his Deputy shall neglect to perform his duty as required by this Act, or commit or suffer to be committed any undue or fraudulent practice in the execution thereof, and be thereof legally convicted, then such Registrar shall forfeit his said office, and shall be liable to pay treble damages, with full costs of suit, to any person or persons that shall be injured thereby."[3]

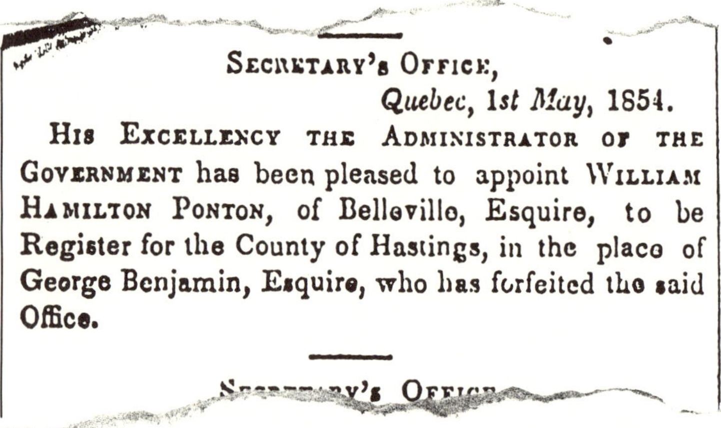

Benjamin was caught by the severity of the new standards,
even though he was not personally aware of any lapse of duty.

The act imposed a very high duty on county registrars. By its wording, it was possible for a registrar to be responsible for a neglect of duty even if he was unaware of it. Bowell's recollection was that an error of a "clerk in the office" for which Benjamin was responsible had triggered the event. Charges were brought against Benjamin in the courts (politically motivated, according to Bowell), and Benjamin was convicted pursuant to the act.[4]

The irony of the situation was inescapable. There had been a dramatic difference in the standards of conduct for county registrars in the eight years since Benjamin had been appointed. Benjamin's predecessor, Allan McLean, had created a public scandal over neglect of duty, a neglect that county council had called "a long and disgraceful delinquency."

McLean had delayed resigning in the face of a public outcry, and, in the wake of his departure in 1846, the Registry Act was amended to include the new standards of conduct, just as Benjamin was being appointed to fill the vacancy. Now Benjamin was caught by the severity of the new standards, even though he was not personally aware of any lapse of duty.

Like McLean, Benjamin had appointed his eldest son, Emanuel Hyman Benjamin, to be deputy registrar in 1851, although Mannie was only 19 at the time. Unlike McLean, George Benjamin had done his best to reorganize the Registry Office and put it back on a businesslike footing. Mannie stayed on in the job after his father's successor, William H. Ponton, was appointed as the new registrar. Following a time-honoured tradition of appointing near relatives to the position, James Ponton, a younger brother of the new registrar, replaced Mannie as deputy registrar shortly afterward.[5] To add insult to injury, the Pontons had a degree of local prominence and were supported by Benjamin's political opponents. William H. Ponton had been elected mayor of Belleville in the three elections between 1851 and 1853.[6] The Pontons were closely allied with Benjamin's rival William Hutton, who regarded them as "entirely respectable, morally and otherwise."[7] Indeed, James Ponton had married Hutton's daughter in 1852.[8]

His reputation stained by the public notice of his dismissal, Benjamin undoubtedly felt he had not been given the support that he deserved from his political friends. When a new general election to the Canadian assembly was called in August 1854, just three months later, George Benjamin announced that he would run in Hastings riding against his political ally, Edmund Murney.

George Benjamin was not the first Jew to seek a seat in a legislature in British North America. Twice before Jews had been elected to provincial legislatures. Neither of them had been allowed to take his seat as a Jew.

The first, Samuel Hart, was elected to the Nova Scotia legislature on 5 March 1793.[9] Although he had been brought up as an observant Jew in Newport, Rhode Island, he discovered after his election that he could not take the oath of office and be seated in the legislature unless he was a Christian. By the time he took the oath of office on 20 March 1793, Hart was indeed a Christian, having had himself baptized at St Paul's Church

(Anglican) in Halifax three days earlier.[10] The second case is that of Ezekiel Hart of Three Rivers.[11] In April 1807 he was elected to the House of Assembly of Lower Canada. When the session commenced in February 1808, he appeared at the bar of the house and requested permission to take his seat. After some debate the French Canadian majority of the assembly resolved on 20 February 1808 "that Ezekiel Hart, Esquire, professing the Jewish Religion, cannot take a seat, nor sit nor vote in this House."[12] In the general Election in May 1808, Hart was again elected to represent Three Rivers in the assembly.

Although Ezekiel Hart had been twice elected by the citizens of Three Rivers, of whom a large majority were French Canadians, he was perceived by the French Canadian members of the assembly as being an addition to the "English Party." When the assembly met next, in April 1809, Hart took the oath of office, kissing the "Holy Evangelist" or New Testament as if he were a Christian, and slipped into his seat.[13] The *Journal* of the assembly records that he actually voted on matters that came before the assembly over a period of two or three weeks.[14] As soon as his presence was noted, however, the assembly again resolved, on 5 May 1809, that as he professed the Jewish religion "he cannot sit or vote in this House," and Hart was again forced to withdraw. He did not allow his name to stand as a candidate in the next general election held in October 1810.

The record in the United States was not much better even though there were many state jurisdictions from which to choose. By 1833, when the Benjamins landed at Toronto, Jacob C. Isacks of Tennessee had been elected to the federal House of Representatives. A Jewish contemporary, writing in England, referred to him as "Mr. Isaacs a Jewish Member of Congress for the State of Tennessee."[15] Yet Isacks' mother was a Christian, he married a Christian, and had other associations with a Christian church.[16] Of the 24 states in the union by 1833, only 5 had elected Jewish representatives to the state legislatures or senates.[17]

Of these elections, the case of Jacob Henry was by far the most dramatic. Henry was elected to the North Carolina House of Commons or Lower House in 1808. When he was re-elected in 1809, an attempt was made to vacate his seat on the ground that "it is contrary to the freedom and independence of our happy and beloved Government, that any person should be allowed to have a seat in this Assembly ... who is not constitutionally qualified for that purpose. It is, therefore, made known that a certain JACOB HENRY, a member of this House, denies the divine authority of the New Testament, and refused to take the Oath prescribed by Law for his qualification, in violation of the constitution of the State." At almost exactly the same date, Henry's case had the opposite conclusion of Ezekiel Hart's in the Lower Canada House of Assembly. Henry made a short but impassioned speech in the state's lower house in which he successfully argued that since the Protestant religion was not enshrined in the constitution of the United States, nor established as a state religion he could not be constitutionally disqualified. "I have never considered it my duty to pry into the belief of other members of his house," he said. "The same *charity*, therefore, it is not unreasonable to expect, will be extended to myself."[18] The opposition melted away, and Jacob Henry kept his seat — with the unanimous support of the House.

George Benjamin was a knowledgeable, informed individual. He was likely aware of the state of development of freedoms in North America. According to his own account, he had lived in North Carolina, though not until almost 20 years after Henry's election. He could not have been unaware of Henry's speech. "Let there be harmony in things essential," ran the motto of Benjamin's *Intelligencer*, "liberality in things not essential," it continued, "*charity* in all," it echoed.[19]

Things had not changed much by 1854. David Levy, the first Jewish senator in the United States, had been elected and had taken office in 1845, after having previously served a term in Congress, although he changed his name to David L. Yulee shortly after his election and was considered "a Jew by race only."[20] Only two Jews had been elected to provincial legislatures in British North America, but neither had been permitted to retain their seats as Jews. Canada had still not seated any Jewish members in its assembly.[21] There had still been no Jew seated in the Parliament of Great Britain. Baron Lionel de Rothschild, elected in 1847, and David Solomons, elected in 1851, were unable to take their seats in the House of Commons without swearing the oaths of office "on the true faith of a Christian," the form required by the Oaths Act. Benjamin Disraeli, who had been a member of the commons since 1837, had been born to Jewish parents, but he had been baptized as a teenager and had sworn the Christian oath of office upon taking his seat.[22] In running against Murney in the Canadian general election, Benjamin, as a Jew, was ready to create another precedent.

Susanna Moodie, on the other hand, was determined to see that he did not. By 1854 she had published her major works and had received recognition as an author. But she still lived in Belleville, her husband was still the sheriff of Hastings County and she had not forgotten her antipathy to George Benjamin, the warden of Hastings County. Through her new English publisher, Richard Bentley, in January 1854 she arranged the publication of her caricature of Benjamin in "Richard Redpath: A Tale" as part of a larger work entitled *Matrimonial speculations*.[23] As Mackenzie Bowell put it, the novelist had "immortalized" the office of the *Intelligencer*.[24] No one was allowed to forget who George Benjamin was or from whence he had come. Susanna Moodie's new book could not have helped him in the election contest in Hastings North.

In 1854, for the first time, Hastings had been split into two: Hastings South, including Belleville, and Hastings North, covering the northern townships that Benjamin was representing so ably as county warden.[25] Billa Flint had decided to leave local politics again and run in Hastings South. Murney, the incumbent in the old Hastings riding, made the decision to run in Hastings North. Benjamin may have had a false sense of his support among the nine townships there. He was by now a proven politician whose support from the north had helped him defeat Flint for the warden's position, even though Flint was a former member of parliament and mayor of Belleville.

There may have been deeper reasons motivating Benjamin to run against Murney. For one thing, the position of registrar was Benjamin's main source of income and now he had lost it. For another, Benjamin no longer owed any loyalty to Murney. Even though it was the Reformers who had secured Benjamin's dismissal, Murney, as member for the past three years, had not done enough to intercede on his behalf. Besides, the Tories were still the government in May 1854, when Benjamin's office was forfeited, and Murney was one of their supporters. Could the government not have had Benjamin reappointed as registrar instead of replacing him with William Ponton? There was nothing in the Registry Act that prevented it.

Benjamin's contest against Murney in Hastings North turned out to be ill-advised. When the votes were counted, Benjamin had lost.[26] And yet, at the annual election for warden of Hastings on 23 January 1855, Benjamin was once again elected, this time without opposition.[27] When he summed up his career in county politics shortly after, he said that it was "gratifying to him to know that many had entered the Council not only as his political but personal enemies, and had left it, with their views and opinions changed with reference to himself. This had been the case frequently during the time he had the honour of being in the Council."[28]

In 1856, when Murney decided to run for election in the division of Trent for the Legislative Council, he first consulted George Benjamin. Their discussion resulted in what the Reform *Hastings Chronicle* bitingly called "a perfect understanding between these two gentlemen." Murney would resign the Hastings North seat that Benjamin had failed to win just two years earlier, and Benjamin would run again in a by-election.

The *Chronicle* had been founded in 1841 by Elijah Miles, the son of a publisher-cum-Wesleyan Methodist minister, as Belleville's reform newspaper.[29] Originally called the *Victoria Chronicle*, it had changed its name to the *Chronicle* in 1850 when the Victoria District was reconstituted as Hastings County, and, following the hiring of Abraham Diamond as editor in 1856, became the area's most effective, if overly enthusiastic, opposition to Benjamin and the Tories.[30] The *Hastings Chronicle* noted that "Mr. Murney has said he will not *oppose* Mr. Benjamin" and inferred that Murney "cannot afford to do so as Mr. B. would oppose him." It followed that when Murney "sold the North Riding to Mr. Benjamin, the price was Mr. B.'s support in the Trent Division."[31]

On 28 October 1856 the *Intelligencer* reported that Benjamin had been elected to the Legislative Assembly over Dr Joshua McLean of Rawdon Township by 987 votes to 341 — a 646 vote majority! "A majority unequalled in this County," the *Intelligencer* noted.[32] The *Chronicle* conceded that "Very few doubted the election of this gentleman, but none anticipated so large a majority."[33] Of approximately 1,800 voters in the riding, more than two-thirds voted, and Benjamin received the support of more than half of those registered. His victory was achieved despite the fact that his Jewish origins were no secret — Susanna Moodie had made certain of that. It was a fact that Benjamin had not been baptized, but to the credit of the electors his religion was not an issue in the election. It was questions of potential annexation to the United States and extending rights to Catholic separate schools that occupied the attention of the electorate. The *Chronicle* was overwhelmed: "Mr. Benjamin by some extraordinary means secured the combined Orange and Catholic vote."

On 26 January 1857, Benjamin took his seat at the meeting of Hastings County Council as reeve of Hungerford Township. He was nominated as warden. He rose to his feet and announced that he would decline the nomination. He was not going to hold more than one elected office at a time. Long before his provincial election, he had decided not to be warden again. He said his greatest task was "getting the Road business of the county finished" and he regretted that there was still more to do. He was satisfied that the credit of the county was well established under 30-year debentures at an interest rate of six and a half percent, "the lowest rate of any other Canadian municipality."[34] He supported Nathaniel S. Appleby of Tyendinaga Township as warden, thereby returning a favour given by Appleby four years earlier when his casting vote had decided Benjamin's own election.[35]

When the assembly resumed sitting at Toronto on 26 February 1857, Benjamin was sworn in as a member of the parliament of the Province of Canada and took his seat on the side of the supporters of John A. Macdonald.[36] He swore his oath of office as a member of the assembly ending with the words "so help me God." He did not swear the oath of abjuration, nor was he asked to.

It had been 200 years since Jews were allowed back to England. There had still been no Jewish member *seated* in the Parliament of Great Britain although two had been *elected* within the last decade without being able to take their seats. But the people of Canada,[37] through the electors of

Hastings North and George Benjamin's successful candidacy, had made history. Benjamin was the first Jew to be elected to the Canadian parliament. He was the first Jew whose right to be seated in a British North American legislature was not contested.

NOTES

1 [Mackenzie Bowell], "George Benjamin, Esq.," *loc. cit.*

2 *Canada Gazette*, 1854, p. 790. William Hamilton Ponton was mayor of Belleville from 1851 to 1853 according to Mika, *op. cit.*, p. 194.

3 The Registry Act (1846), 9 Victoria, c. 24, section 21.

4 The trial was held at the assizes in Belleville, probably before Justice William Henry Draper, in 1854, although the records have not been located. It is likely that the charges had been laid against Benjamin in 1851 as Bowell recalled that Benjamin was "dismissed by the Baldwin La Fontaine Ministry," his political opponents, who had in fact gone out of office in August 1851. It was Draper's conservative government that had appointed Benjamin to the position of registrar in 1846. Draper had resigned on 28 May 1847 to become judge of the Court of Queen's Bench. He later became Chief Justice of the Court of Appeal. George Metcalf, "William Henry Draper," *Dictionary of Canadian Biography*, vol. X.

5 Information on file at the Hastings County Registry Office. Both Pontons continued to hold office until 1889.

6 Nick and Helma Mika, *Mosaic of Belleville* (Belleville, Mika Silk Screening Limited, 1966), p. 194.

7 Gerald Boyce, *Hutton of Hastings* (Belleville, Hastings County Council, 1972), p. 176. The Pontons, sons of Dr Mungo Ponton (d. 1849), had come to Belleville from Scotland about 1834.

8 *Ibid.*

9 Samuel Hart (1749-1810), son of Jacob Hart and Esther Levy, was born in Newport, Rhode Island. The writ for the election was issued 22 January 1793 and returned 20 March 1793. *The Legislative Assembly of Nova Scotia 1758-1983: a biographical directory*, ed. Shirley B. Elliott, pp. 255-56. The election actually took

place on 4 March 1793 and Hart was declared elected at that time. *The diary of Simeon Perkins, 1790-1796*, ed. Charles Bruce Fergusson (Toronto, Champlain Society, 1961), entry of 4 March 1793.

10 "St. Paul's Church Baptismal Record" in the Anglican Diocesan Centre, Halifax, N. S., "Bapt'd March 17 [1793] Mr. Samuel Hart, Merchant, an Adult."

11 Ezekiel Hart (1770-1843) was the second son of Aaron Hart, who had settled in Quebec in 1760.

12 "Proceedings Relating to the Expulsion of Ezekiel Hart from the House of Assembly of Lower Canada," *Journals*, 1808 and 1809, reprinted in A. G. Doughty and D. A. MacArthur, *Documents relating to the constitutional history of Canada, 1791-1818*, pp. 351-65. *See also* "Early Hart Papers" in the McCord Museum, files 61 (M18648), 62 (M18647), and 63 (Ezekiel Hart to Jonas Phillips and Sons, May 26, 1808); B. G. Sack, *History of the Jews in Canada*, vol. I (Montreal, Canadian Jewish Congress, 1945), pp. 80-95.

13 The actual oath of a member of the assembly, unlike the Oath of Abjuration, did not contain the concluding words "on the true faith of a Christian" and should not therefore have been offensive to a professing Jew. The original oaths, signed by Hart, are in NAC, RGl, E 11, vols. 2 and 10.

14 *See* David Rome, "On the Early Harts," *Canadian Jewish Archives, new series*, vols. 16-18 (Montreal, Canadian Jewish Congress, 1980), pp. 328-54.

15 F. H. Goldsmid, *The arguments advanced against the enfranchisement of the Jews* (Second Edition, London, 1833), app. II.

16 *Biographical directory of the American Congress, 1774-1971*, p. 1174. Jacob C. Isacks was born in Montgomery County, Pennsylvania, in 1767 to Jacob Isacks and Magdelena Cope. He was married to Martha Bullard, a Christian. He died in Winchester, Tenn., in 1835 after donating a tract of land for the construction of a Protestant church. *Biographical directory of the Tennessee General Assembly*, vol. I, 1796-1861 (Nashville, Tennessee State Library, 1975), pp. 398-99.

17 App. II in F. H. Goldsmid, *op. cit. See also Publications: American Jewish Historical Society*, 12 (1904), pp. 163-64. There were undoubtedly other Jewish parliamentarians in the American state legislatures: Ephraim Hart (1747-1825) became a New York State senator in 1810 (G. N. Hart, "Ephraim Hart," *PAJHS*, 4 (1896), pp. 215-18). David Emanuel (1744-1808) was elected to the Georgia assembly in 1783 and became the state's sixth governor in 1801, although he may have been a Jew by ancestry only (Leon Huhner, "The First Jew to Hold the Office of Governor of One of the United States," *PAJHS*, 17 (1909), pp. 187-95).

18 Ira Rosenwaike, "Further Light on Jacob Henry" (pp. 47-51) and "Jacob Henry's Speech, 1809" (pp. 43-46), *Jews in the South*, ed. Leonard Dinnerstein and Mary Dale Palsson (Baton Rouge, Louisiana State Press, 1973). Henry was born about

1775 and died in 1847. According to contemporary reports, his speech had been written by State Chief Justice John Louis Taylor.

[19] Emphasis added by the authors.

[20] David Levy (1810-86) was elected to the Senate as the first senator of the State of Florida upon its admission to the union in 1845. He had previously served in Congress as a delegate from Florida Territory (1841-45). He changed his name to David L. Yulee upon his marriage to Miss Wickliffe shortly after his election to the Senate. He was defeated in his attempt to be re-elected in 1851, but served a further term as senator (1855-61). According to his biographer, he was "a Jew by race only." Leon Huhner, "David L. Yulee, Florida's First Senator," *PAJHS*, 25 (1917), pp. 1-29, reprinted in *Jews in the South, op. cit.*, pp. 52-74.

[21] In September 1843 Henry Hague Judah (1808-83) was elected in a by-election to represent the riding of Champlain in the Legislative Assembly of the new Province of Canada. Joseph Desjardins, *Guide parlementaire historique de la Province de Québec 1792 à 1902* (Québec, Bibliotheque de la Legislature de Québec, 1902), p. 155. Though his father, Henry Judah, was born and raised as a Jew, his mother, Jane More, was a Christian. Judah himself was likely baptized at his birth, and raised as a Christian. The older children of Henry and Jane Judah, born in Lower Canada, were baptized as Protestants: Eleanor Wortley on 4 January 1803, John Young on 6 May 1804 (d. 24 July 1804), and Thomas Storrs, born 8 December 1805. ANQ, Index of Protestant births, baptisms, and deaths. After Henry Hague Judah's death in 1883, he was recalled as "one of the pillars of the Anglican communion." T. Taggart Smyth, *The first hundred years* (Montreal, Montreal City and District Savings Bank, Montreal, 1946), p. 77. For biographical material on Judah see: David Rome, *Canadian Jewish Archives, new series*, no. 20 (Montreal, Canadian Jewish Congress, 1981), pp. 137-43, 184, 199, 153, 217-25. His obituary was published in *La Minerve* (Montreal), 12 February 1883.

[22] Benjamin Disraeli, Earl of Beaconsfield (1804-81) was born in London, England to Isaac and Miriam D'Israeli, both Jews whose families were of Italian origin. In 1814 Isaac D'Israeli was elected warden of the Bevis Marks Synagogue but declined the office and was fined £40. D'Israeli refused to pay the fine and broke off all formal connections with the community. Though he never converted to Christianity, his sons did. Benjamin Disraeli was baptized in 1817 at the age of 14. First elected to the House of Commons in 1837, he became leader of the Conservatives in the House of Commons for a few months in 1858, and again from 1865 to 1868, when he became prime minister. He was out of office from 1869 to 1874. He again became prime minister in 1874 and continued in that position from 1876 to 1880 in the House of Lords as the Earl of Beaconsfield: *The Jewish encyclopedia* (N. Y. and London, Funk and Wagnalls Co., 1925), vol. 4, pp. 618-22; Lucien Wolf, "The Disraeli Family," *Jewish Historical Society of England Transactions*, 5 (1908) (reprinted by William Dawson and Sons, 1971), pp. 202-18.

23 Ballstadt *et al.*, *op cit.*, pp. 88-89 and 147.

24 *Ibid.*, quoting Mackenzie Bowell in "The Old Office," 26 December 1862. *See also* "The Intelligencer Office, An Old Landmark, Corner of Front & Bridge Streets," *Intelligencer*, 1 April 1872, p. 2, col. 4.

25 16 Victoria II, c. 152 (1853), section 7.

26 [Bowell], "George Benjamin, Esq.," *loc. cit.*

27 Victoria District *Records and Proceedings*, vol. II, pp. 610-11. Part of the reason for Benjamin's easy triumph as warden was undoubtedly the fact that Billa Flint, having been returned for Hastings South in the 1854 election, was no longer on county council.

28 *Intelligencer*, 28 January 1857.

29 H. P. Gundy, "Stephen Miles," *Dictionary of Canadian Biography*, vol. IX.

30 Abraham Diamond (1828-80), a Wesleyan Methodist of loyalist descent, edited the *Hastings Chronicle* from 1856 to 1868. Elwood Jones, "Abraham Diamond," *Dictionary of Canadian Biography*, vol. X.

31 *Hastings Chronicle*, 8 October 1856, p. 2, cols. 3-5.

32 *Intelligencer*, 28 October 1856. McLean, a physician, died 18 December 1858 at the village of Stirling. *See* PAO, A410, will probated 26 January 1859, County of Hastings. McLean does not appear to have been related to Allan McLean.

33 *Hastings Chronicle*, 22 October 1856, p. 2, col. 4.

34 *Intelligencer*, 27 January 1857.

35 Victoria District *Records and Proceedings*, vol. II, p. 507 ff.

36 There is a lack of clarity involving the use of the term Parliament in the Province of Canada in the period from 1841 to 1867. According to section 2 of the British Act to Reunite the Provinces of Upper and Lower Canada, and for the government of Canada (3 & 4 Vic., c. 35), known by its short title as the Union Act of 1840, representative government in the new Province of Canada was to be embodied in a popularly elected Legislative Assembly as well as an appointed Legislative Council (the latter was subsequently altered to provide for the election of some of its members). Notwithstanding these official titles, the Legislative Assembly was popularly known as the House of Assembly or, more commonly, as simply the House, and the Legislative Council was known as the Upper House. The term Parliament was widely used in both government documents and newspaper accounts to describe the House of Assembly, and in some cases as a collective noun to describe both houses. The Union Act fell short of specifying whether a person elected to the House was to be referred to as "Member of the Legislative Assembly" (MLA) or as "Member of the Provincial Par-

liament" (MPP). On the basis of newspaper accounts, both terms appear to have been used. See for example, "The Huntingdon and Hungerford Celebration in North Hastings," *Intelligencer*, 28 November 1856, which refers to "George Benjamin, Esq., MPP" and his recent election to "Parliament."

[37] The Province of Canada after the Union Act continued to be one of the colonies or provinces of British North America, similar in status to the smaller provinces of Nova Scotia, New Brunswick, Prince Edward Island, and Newfoundland. In fact, however, the Province of Canada was an experimental union of the old provinces of Upper and Lower Canada, roughly corresponding to the present day provinces of Ontario and Quebec. Though the united province retained most of the separate legal, procedural, and linguistic distinctions of each of its former parts, it had a single parliamentary system.

CHAPTER IX

The Homecoming

ॐ

> "Until I went home in 1857, I had not received a letter from
> England for years. They gradually dropped off. I once wrote
> home about it and as I guess pretty sharply telling them that I
> did not credit the plea of want of time, that no matter what a per-
> son had to do, one who use[s] a ready pen could always find
> time to write absent relatives. To this I rec'd no answer."
>
> *George Benjamin, 6 May 1864*

THE SESSION OF THE LEGISLATURE FOR 1857 CONCLUDED ON 10 JUNE. FOR Benjamin, this, his first session as member for North Hastings, had been a resounding success. He had introduced seven bills, more than all but six other members. Three bills had actually been passed,[1] including a bill for the safety of railways, introduced after the disastrous railway accident at the Desjardins Canal near Dundas on 12 March when a bridge collapsed and 59 people were killed.[2]

Notwithstanding his experience as an Orangeman, he knew that he would need the support of Catholics to have success in parliament. His leadership role in the Orange movement had ended the previous year and was not to be taken up. He had spoken in favour of the French Canadians during the debate on the seat of government in March.[3] He voted with the French Canadians in supporting the Loretto Bill for the incorporation of a Roman Catholic seminary.[4] "The French are your sheet anchor," John A. Macdonald would confide to him later, "you are popular with them."[5] Although his support for Roman Catholic causes was not designed to increase his popularity in North Hastings, Benjamin's overwhelming support by his constituency gave him some comfort in dealing with unpopular causes. Just before the summer it was announced that Benjamin had been appointed a commissioner of the peace, the first appointment of a Jew as a justice of the peace in Canada West.[6]

Benjamin was still in debt. The mortgages owing to George Filliter and George Romanes were still outstanding, but his income had increased as a member of parliament, even though he was no longer warden. In parliament his salary was up to $1,000 per year as a member, in addition to a mileage allowance and generous fees for sitting on committees when parliament was not in session.[7] He still had his 22-room mansion between the Dundas Highway and the bay.[8] Besides Isabella, her 80-year-old mother and himself, by 1857 the Benjamins had ten surviving

George Benjamin, oil painting by William Sawyer, 1859.

children, Isabella Jr, William, and Robert having been born since 1850.[9]

Benjamin was now almost 58 years old himself. Work was winding down for the summer. The fifth legislature of the Province of Canada had been elected in the summer of 1854. By law there was to be an election by the summer of 1858, although the chances were it would be held sometime during the next few months. John A. Macdonald, the leader of the government party in the house, had been authorized to lead an official government mission to London over the summer. In order to allow him to negotiate further support for the Grand Trunk Railway, the Executive Council had authorized him "to call to his aid the services of any gentleman whom he may deem necessary to the support of the negotiations."[10] Benjamin had cut off his ties with his family when he had left England years before, although he had returned home once, in 1851.[11] Somehow, this seemed like a good time to return home again.[12]

Returning to England as a member of the Canadian legislature, Benjamin could not have failed to notice the debate going on that summer over whether Jews should sit in the House of Commons at Westminster. There had been a general election in Britain that April, and Baron de Rothschild had been re-elected as one of the City of London members of parliament — the tenth consecutive year he had been a member without a seat. Lord Palmerston, the prime minister, introduced an amendment to the Oaths Act which would have allowed Jews to sit and vote in Parliament, by removing the words "on the faith of a Christian" as a qualification. The bill carried in the commons but was rejected in the House of Lords.[13] Parliament stayed in session for most of the summer, and the debate continued. The commons considered introducing a new bill to circumvent the House of Lords' position by introducing a resolution specifically allowing Baron de Rothschild to take his seat.[14] It would not, in fact, be until the next year that the British Parliament would pass a law admitting de Rothschild to be the first Jew seated in the House of Commons — a law that had been passed in Canada 25 years earlier.[15]

When Benjamin reached Brighton he found only 3 of his 11 brothers and sisters still at home. His father and mother were long since deceased. His brother Abraham Cohen was married and living in Australia. He had ten children, one of whom, Henry Emanuel, would later become the first

Jewish high-court judge and cabinet minister in New South Wales.[16] George's brother Ralph, who had not married, had followed Abraham to Australia. His sister Martha had married Henry Solomon, a watchmaker, who had become a civic employee and been appointed chief constable of Brighton in 1838. On the evening of 13 March 1844 he had been murdered in his office by an unbalanced youth who had been arrested for stealing a carpet. He had been vice-president of Emanuel Hyam Cohen's Congregation at the time of his murder. Thousands of people had come to his funeral, but he had died penniless and left his widow with ten children.[17] George's sister Zipporah, or Zippy as the family called her, also a widow, was living in London.[18] His brother Benjamin, a physician living

*Benjamin's brother-in-law, Henry Solomon, died
tragically while Benjamin was living in Belleville.*

in New York in reduced circumstances, had only minimal contact with the family.[19]

Levy, Nathan, and Rose were the only ones left in Brighton. Levy Emanuel Cohen, George Benjamin's older brother and owner of the Brighton *Guardian*, had become a recluse. He was near the end of his life, suffering from diabetes.[20] Younger brother Nathan, a bachelor as well, had succeeded Levy as editor of the *Guardian*. George's sister, Rosetta — the family called her Rose — had never married and had taken her turn at running the *Guardian* as well. She was only three years younger than George and was the closest to him.

The family were shocked by the change in George's appearance since his visit seven or eight years earlier. "He has grown so immensely stout," wrote Rosetta, "that we did not any of us know him."[21] At the same time they could not help but be impressed with the progress he had made in his career. "He appears to be doing very well in Canada," Nathan wrote to brother Abraham in Sydney. "He is M.P., if you please, for Hastings, and often sends me papers containing his speeches in the Assembly, where he seems to maintain a high position and exercise considerable influence."[22] George Benjamin was back in touch with his roots. He resolved to keep up the communication.

When Benjamin arrived home in Belleville after the summer, Isabella was pregnant again.[23] Another election was imminent. George and Isabella had decided to enroll their third son, Lewis Nathan, now almost 16, in Upper Canada College in Toronto.[24] Benjamin would be able to see him during sittings of the legislature. The fact that Toronto was currently the seat of government was fortunate. After the Parliament Buildings were burned in Montreal in 1849, representatives of the two regions of the Province of Canada had worked out an arrangement of moving the seat of government back and forth between Toronto and Quebec every four years. This meant that not only the government offices and supporting bureaucracy would have to be moved, but also the legislature. Toronto had been the seat of government since 1856. Even though a compromise had been worked out earlier in the year to build a permanent seat of government in Ottawa, that project could not be completed for some time, and the government was still scheduled to move to Quebec by 1860. The railway had joined Toronto and Montreal through Belleville in 1856. Benjamin could still make the trip to Toronto by horse and carriage, but the trip to Quebec would be much longer. Benjamin therefore came to a decision: this was his last term in parliament. He would not run for re-election, but would try to get a position that would give him a secure income.

He sent off a note to John A. Macdonald asking him for help and telling him he would not run again. By the end of October 1857, Macdonald had still not acknowledged Benjamin's note or suggested a position for him to retire upon. Benjamin wrote again, this time more specifically. The position of collector of customs at Toronto was available. It was just the kind of position he needed. It allowed the collector to keep a portion of the revenue raised and would provide a secure income. Still better, the appointment could be made directly by Macdonald's ministry.[25]

Macdonald answered from Toronto on 4 November. He was unwilling to accept Benjamin's retirement. "So get ready like a good fellow," he said. " I won't listen to your retiring into private life, until you have returned to your constituents and got their approbation. Do not be a horse for *one heat* only."[26] The position of customs collector was not available, Macdonald continued, because the Civil Service Bill would prevent it.[27] Then came the words Benjamin was waiting for. "After by the aid of yourself & others, we are firmly in the Saddle for 4 years I am quite ready to see that you are provided for in a manner suitable to your standing & gratifying to your friends — I mentioned several contingencies to you — all of which will be available at the right time."[28] Macdonald's letter then ran on for a few pages of speculation about the election being expected within a month or so, of suggestions about the potential candidates, of discussion about the issues. "However enough of this," Macdonald concluded abruptly. "Burn this gossip."

Benjamin was certainly not going to burn it. The letter contained a lot of chit chat, but some of Macdonald's words stood out clearly. Macdonald had said "I won't listen to your retiring into private life." He had said that if Benjamin ran again and if Macdonald's party was in control of the Government — "firmly in the Saddle for 4 years" was how he put it — he

John Alexander Macdonald, c. 1863,
Co-Premier of the Province of Canada.
"However enough of this," Macdonald concluded abruptly,
"Burn this gossip."

was "quite ready to see that you are provided for in a manner suitable to your standing and gratifying to your friends."

Macdonald's words contained two qualifications. The first was a condition that Benjamin had to help him by running again if he wanted a satisfactory position for retirement. The second was worth further consideration, particularly the "firmly in the Saddle for 4 years" line. Could that possibly have meant that Macdonald couldn't promise Benjamin anything unless he won a majority government? Macdonald had not said that at all. He had simply stated the obvious: that he could not give Benjamin a position unless it was in his power to do so.

And there was more. Macdonald recalled mentioning "several contingencies ... all of which will be available at the right time." For a man who had spent much of his working life as a newspaper editor, the wording was significant. Macdonald had said "will be available," not "would be available." Benjamin would have taken this as a clear-cut promise.

By the time the writ of election was issued on 28 November, Benjamin had decided to run again. But he would retire as soon as the new government was settled. He would not run for reeve of Hungerford or warden of Hastings.

NOTES

1 "The Last Session," *Intelligencer*, 10 July 1857.

2 George Benjamin, "To the Independent Electors of Hastings North," *ibid.*, 4 December 1857.

3 "The Seat of Government," *ibid.*, 27 March 1857.

4 Benjamin, *loc. cit.*, 4 December 1857.

5 Macdonald to G. Benjamin, 4 June 1861, in *The papers of the prime ministers, volume II. The letters of Sir John A. Macdonald, 1858-1861*, ed. J. K. Johnson and Carole B. Stelmack, p. 342.

6 *Intelligencer*, 14 August 1857.

7 "Mr Benjamin's Assertions," *Hastings Chronicle*, 27 March 1861.

8 Ruby Milburn, a grand-daughter of George and Isabella Benjamin, remembered the house as "a very large house about 22 rooms built on the Dundas Highway and the property extended south to the shore line. The Deacon Shirt Factory is now built where the house was. Well away from the house was a cook house where they smoked hams. There was cane sugar which was strung on string ... ." "George Benjamin File," Belleville Public Library. The original house was demolished by 1942, when the Deacon Shirt factory was built. The present address is 121 Dundas Street East.

9 St. Thomas' Church records, *loc. cit.* Isabella Georgia Pauline, born 11 November
   1851, baptized 25 January 1852, register no. 7-B-3, p. 418; William Francis Hill,
   born 20 October 1853; and Robert Hinden, born 13 February 1856. Information
   on the latter two from "George C. Benjamin's Family Record," p. 5.

10 Donald Creighton, *John A. Macdonald: the young politician* (Toronto, MacMillan,
    1956), pp. 253-54. John Rose of Montreal accompanied Macdonald on the mis-
    sion. Though there is no documentary evidence to confirm that Benjamin was part
    of the official delegation, it is known that he was in England at the same time and
    that his inclusion in the delegation would have been consistent with his personal
    circumstances and his standing in his party.

11 Rosetta Cohen, Brighton, to Abraham Cohen, Sydney, N. S. W., 12 March 1852,
    Abraham Cohen family papers in the possession of the family, Sydney, Australia.
    "We had a letter from our dear brother Mo ... . I hope dear Aby you will not fail to
    write to him, for he tells me he wrote two letters to you soon after he returned
    home from his visit to us and he feels hurt that you did not answer them."

12 George Benjamin to Abraham Cohen, Sydney, 6 May 1864, Abraham Cohen fam-
    ily papers, *loc. cit.* There is conflicting evidence regarding the date of Benjamin's
    visit to Brighton. In the letter indicated, Benjamin states explicitly that he visited
    home in 1857. In other correspondence in the Abraham Cohen family papers,
    there is a suggestion by Benjamin's sister Rosetta that the visit took place in 1858
    in the following words: "I must tell you dear Aby that we had a visit from our dear
    Brother Mo last summer.": Rosetta Cohen to Abraham Cohen, 17 January 1859,
    ibid. The 1857 date is regarded as more likely as Benjamin was recorded as being
    in Canada during the summer of 1858. During that year, the assembly sat through
    most of the summer until the session ended on Monday 16 August. Benjamin was
    present throughout the session and took part in recorded votes at least as late as
    August 13: *Legislative Assembly Journals*, 1858, vol. II, p. 1030.

13 In the House of Commons the bill carried by 291 to 168; in the House of Lords it
    was rejected by a vote of 171 to 139. *See* Henry S. Q. Henriques, "The Political
    Rights of English Jews, Part II," *Jewish Quarterly Review*, XIX (1907), pp. 751-91 at
    pp. 767-72. *See also Hansard*, Parliamentary Debates, vol. 146, pp. 143-48, 347-65.
    In fact, this was the second time the House of Commons had passed a bill amend-
    ing the Oaths Act for the purpose of admitting Jews as members of Parliament.
    The first successful attempt, the previous year, was passed by 159 votes to 110, but
    rejected by the House of Lords 110 votes to 78. *Ibid.*, pp. 766-67.

14 The resolution passed first reading but did not proceed. Meanwhile, there was
    some speculation that Baron de Rothschild would force the issue by attempting to
    take his seat and obtaining a resolution from the house allowing him to omit the

obnoxious words. This would have inevitably caused a collision between the House of Commons and the law courts. *Ibid.*, pp. 770-71.

15 The Province of Lower Canada passed a law admitting Jews to full equality with Christians as 1 William IV, c. 57, in 1831. It received royal assent on 12 April 1832. The Province of Upper Canada had passed its amendment to the Oaths Act as 3 William IV, c. 12 (1833), which had the same effect.

16 For further reading on Abraham Cohen (1811/12-74), see David J. Benjamin, "Henry Emanuel Cohen," *Australian Jewish Historical Society*, II (1948), pp. 524-61.

17 David Spector, *op. cit.*, p. 45. *See also* Martha Solomons, Brighton, to Abraham and Sophia Cohen, Sydney, 27 June 1850, Abraham Cohen family papers.

18 Henry Robert Cohen, " Summary of the Abraham Cohen Family in Australia," notes on file in the *Australian Jewish Historical Society*, Sydney, N. S. W.

19 Rosetta Cohen to Abraham Cohen, 17 January, 1859, Abraham Cohen family papers.

20 Benjamin W. Cohen to Abraham Cohen, 26 August, 1862, Abraham Cohen family papers.

21 "Zip has the same complaint as poor Levy had, The diabets, and unfortunately the Doctors cannot do much for her." Rosetta Cohen to Abraham Cohen, 24 July 1864, Abraham Cohen family papers, *loc. cit.*, Levy Emanuel Cohen died on 7 November 1860. Brighton *Guardian*, 21, 28 November 1860, reprinted in the London *Jewish Chronicle*, November 1860, pp. 2-41.

22 Nathan Cohen to Abraham Cohen, 17 January 1859, Abraham Cohen family papers.

23 Rosetta Julia, born 13 March 1858. George C. Benjamin's family record, *op. cit.*, p. 6.

24 *Roll of pupils of Upper Canada College*, p. 108.

25 Macdonald to Benjamin, 4 November 1857, Benjamin family papers.

26 *Ibid.*

27 "An Act for improving the organization and increasing the efficiency of the Civil Service of Canada," 20 Victoria, c. 24 (passed 10 June 1857). The act provided for the first time that appointments to designated positions in the service of the government of Canada, including the position of customs collector, were to be made only after examinations of applicants by a board of examiners composed of several sen-

ior government employees at the deputy ministerial level. The act also provided a scale of remuneration of customs collectors based upon annual revenue collected at the port of entry concerned, with the highest annual salary of £750 going to the customs collector at a port with annual revenue of over £250,000, such as Toronto. The salary for the customs collector at Belleville would have been in the range of £350 to £400 per year based upon its annual volume.

[28] Macdonald to Benjamin, 4 November 1857, *loc. cit.*

CHAPTER X

The Promise

> "You had said in your letter to me, that at the close of the
> session you would give me such an appointment to retire upon,
> as would please my friends and sustain my position."
>
> *George Benjamin to John A. Macdonald, 28 March 1858*

JUST BEFORE THE FIRST SESSION OF THE SIXTH LEGISLATURE OF THE PROVINCE of Canada opened in Toronto on 25 February 1858, George Benjamin met his leader, the Honourable John A. Macdonald.[1] Benjamin had been re-elected in Hastings North in the general elections on 24 and 26 December 1857, but with his majority slashed to only 125 votes — "within the bounds of possible defeat" was how the *Hastings Chronicle* phrased it.[2] He had run against Philip Luke, the reeve of Huntingdon Township, a moderate Conservative and proprietor of Luke's Tavern.[3]

Luke's political strength was in the north part of Hastings County and he made the most of it. He had reminded the electorate that Benjamin did not live in North Hastings, but in Belleville. He charged that Benjamin as warden had run the county into debt for the construction of roads and that Benjamin "made a living out of these roads."[4] He tried to rally the Orange Protestant voters against Benjamin for supporting the bill for the incorporation of the Sisters of Loretto, which had passed the legislature during the previous session. In that support the *Hastings Chronicle* decided Benjamin had "trifled with the principles upon which he was elected."[5] Some of Luke's more overzealous supporters had actually circulated a broadside entitled "the Nunnery," which attacked Benjamin

as a supporter of Roman Catholics.[6] But Mackenzie Bowell had finessed
the Orange opposition in a very innovative way. He had written to the
current grand master of the Orange lodges, George L. Allan in Toronto,
and asked him for his "opinion of the vote upon the Bill for the
Incorporation of the Sisters of Loretto, given by Bro. George Benjamin,
as to whether he did *right* or *wrong.*"[7] Allan's answer, which Bowell
published in the *Intelligencer*, completely exonerated Benjamin. "I do not
see" said Allan, "how he could lay the slightest claim to that spirit of
toleration which is exhibited in our general declaration and qualification
as an Orangemen, did he vote otherwise." That said, Allan felt obliged
to add his own caveat: "Of course, I would be exceedingly sorry to send
any child or relation of mine to such an Institution, well knowing the
imposing nature which Romanish formularies possess for youthful
minds."[8] Bowell's editorial then took up the argument: "Let every
Protestant ask this simple question" he continued explaining the motivation of Benjamin's vote on the Loretto Bill, "should we not give the
Roman Catholics the same *rights*, Civil, Religious and Political, that we
ourselves enjoy?"[9]

George Benjamin knew the meaning of prejudice from his own
personal experience and ancestral memory — the question of equal rights
for Jews had confronted his people for centuries. His support of the
Loretto Bill was his way of working towards the development of freedoms
for all people in Canada. That was his driving force. He was not "trifling
with the principles upon which he was elected" as the *Hastings Chronicle*
said.[10] He was advancing those principles on which Canada is founded
today.

When the election was over Benjamin had once again held enough
Catholic and Protestant supporters to retain his seat. The *Hastings
Chronicle's* bitter assessment of the victory was that he had been saved
only by "the Northern Hordes," that many of his voters were falsely
registered "men residing out of the county who knew him not."[11] Actually
Benjamin had fared much better in the election than had many of
Macdonald's other Conservative supporters. Three of his cabinet ministers, William Cayley, Robert Spence, and Joseph Curran Morrison, were
defeated. While Macdonald himself was easily re-elected in Kingston, his

party was devastated in Canada West and held a slim apparent majority only because of the large gains made by the supporters of his ally, George-Étienne Cartier, among the French-speaking voters of Canada East. In this election, George Brown, owner of the Toronto *Globe* and leader of the radicals or Grits, had emerged as the dominant force among the Liberals of Canada West.[12]

Just after the new year, Benjamin wrote to Macdonald and reminded him about his promise of an office to retire upon. At the same time, Macdonald was faced with the delicate task of rebuilding a majority in the legislature in order to retain power when the session resumed in late February. He relied heavily on Benjamin as one of his remaining elected supporters in the area between Kingston and Toronto, and accepted him in the role of lieutenant or whip to feel out independent members and obtain their support for the anticipated motion of want of confidence by the opposition.[13] In these circumstances, Macdonald renewed his promise to Benjamin that he would find him an appointment adequate to retire upon.[14]

Benjamin had every reason to trust Macdonald. His Son Emanuel Hyman Benjamin had been appointed by Macdonald to a position in the postal service during the last session and now worked for the government in Toronto.[15] When they met in Toronto at the end of February, Macdonald repeated his promise. Macdonald told him there was to be a joint commission appointed to inquire into the state of the prisons and that Benjamin would be one of the two commissioners. The joint commission would recommend appointments to positions for supervisors of the prisons. The previous year, at Macdonald's direction, Benjamin had prepared prison bills, which had passed during the last session and authorized the appointment of five prison inspectors for Canada — a chief and four subordinates. There was a possible appointment there for Benjamin. Another possibility was paymaster of the police, a position proposed in the police bill being introduced by Sir Allan McNab.[16]

Somehow, over the first month of the session, all these possibilities evaporated. The bill for the joint commission on prisons failed as did McNab's bill. The positions of inspector of prisons were still possible, but the subordinates had salaries of only £350 a year, on which amount Benjamin said "I could not keep my family much less educate and bring them up." That left only the job of chief inspector, but Macdonald mentioned to Benjamin that he was going to send away for a chief from England or the United States.[17]

At the same time the position of customs collector at Toronto, which had not been available to Benjamin the previous November because of the Civil Service Bill,[18] was now given to Robert Spence, who had been the postmaster general in Macdonald's government until he was defeated in the election.[19] Then Benjamin heard that Macdonald was trying to arrange an increase in the salary of the custom's officer at Belleville so it would be suitable for Benjamin.[20] He was beginning to understand that nothing imminent was going to happen regarding Macdonald's promise, and that there were no satisfactory appointments in the offing. It was Friday, 25 March 1858. Isabella had given birth to another daughter, Rosetta Julia, on 13 March, not two weeks earlier.[21] Benjamin had planned to go home for the weekend. Suddenly he decided he had to talk to Macdonald first. He went to Macdonald's office but someone else came in, and he had to leave without saying what was on his mind. He drafted a letter to Macdonald over the weekend and delivered it on Monday. He set out all the circumstances and then concluded: "If I am going out of Parliament and God knows I wish it, [and if] it [your promise] is all a delusion, I should know at once, and I much desire to leave where I am. Places are vacant, and are daily becoming vacant, which I could fill, but I point out none."[22]

There was no doubt Macdonald was preoccupied with other things. During March he had been depressed by illness and a sense of personal loss, as well as by the constant reminder of his political setback every time he faced George Brown in the legislature. In March, Macdonald confided to his sister that he wanted to retire.[23] As the session wore on his ability to find an appointment for Benjamin became more and more constricted. At the end of July his government was defeated and forced to resign. Brown, the leader of the Grits, could have insisted on a new election but he was asked to form a government and accepted. As it turned out, he was overconfident and his new government was defeated on 4 August and in turn forced to resign. Macdonald's Conservatives were again asked to form a government, with Brown in opposition. The event became immortalized as the "double shuffle."[24] By the time the session ended two weeks later, Macdonald was in apparent control, but he had had his hands full. He had not found Benjamin an appointment.

Macdonald clung to power for the next three years leading what would later be known as a minority government. The party system was much less definable than it was a century later. Macdonald's party, the Liberal-Conservative coalition, was a combination of Conservatives, the descendants of the "establishment," as well as a large number of moderate reformers who had, ironically, been Macdonald's opponents a decade earlier. But by far the greatest number of Macdonald's supporters were the *Parti Bleu* of Canada East, who came to him through his co-leader of the ministry, George-Étienne Cartier. In opposition there were at least two or three distinct factions of Liberals. There were the Clear Grits of Canada West, led by George Brown; a group of French-speaking *Parti Rouge* members from Canada East, led by Antoine-Aimé Dorion; and finally a small group of Liberal members led by John Sandfield Macdonald.

In these circumstances John A. Macdonald was forced to compromise on virtually every measure the government tried to introduce and was unable to have his supporters appointed to offices without the scrutiny of the opposition, and the danger of another defeat of the government. Benjamin could not expect him to keep his promise for the present. None the less, he remained loyal to Macdonald, supporting his party at every occasion. But their relationship cooled noticeably, and Benjamin decided to take steps to make himself less vulnerable. He decided to go back into municipal politics while continuing to hold his seat in the legislature. At the elections for council of Hungerford Township in January 1859, he was elected after an absence of a year, and was appointed reeve of the township by the new council. On 25 January he appeared at the county-council meeting. He knew most of the county councillors. Nathaniel Appleby, reeve of Tyendinaga Township, had been warden for the past two years. Billa Flint, who had left county politics during his three years as member of the legislature for Hastings South, had not run in the general election of 1857 and was now reeve of Elzevir Township. Flint moved that Caleb Gilbert of Sidney be warden, while A. F. Wood of Madoc moved that Benjamin be warden. Then Appleby was nominated, but declined, with the result that Benjamin became warden of Hastings by a vote of ten to two.

In accepting the position, he said he had returned to municipal politics because "he was actuated by no other motive than the advancement of the Marmora Railway," and that he could do more to promote it as warden than he could as an outsider.[25] The statement, at face value, was a logical one. As warden in 1855, he had been responsible for ensuring that the Marmora Iron Foundry raised sufficient capital from the public to commence operation. His plan was that the foundry would help in the development of Marmora Township and would make Hastings "the Chief Manufacturing District in Canada."[26] Now the Belleville and Marmora Railway was proposed to handle the vast amount of business to be generated at the foundry and to provide a railway link with the rest of the Canadian transportation network. In this way, he had said, "all would feel in a direct manner the growing prosperity of the county."[27]

But Benjamin's underlying reason for returning to municipal politics was undoubtedly his disappointment at the lack of an appointment to a position through his contacts in the government of Canada. He was approaching his 60th birthday that March, and he needed to keep his options open. Benjamin's opponents felt he had come back to the county council because of the money. One letter to the *Hastings Chronicle*, signed "Ratepayer," charged that, as warden, he was not having county printing contracts performed by the lowest bidder, but was having them awarded to the *Intelligencer* without giving other printers the opportunity to bid. "Ratepayer" noted that "Benjamin is now paid $500 per year as warden, from $600 to $1000 per year as representative of the North Riding in Parliament, besides his mileage. He has also got several thousand dollars from the public treasury attending on two or three party committees."[28]

Benjamin was frantically busy for the first two months of 1860. He was re-elected as reeve of Hungerford and warden in January. Isabella gave birth to another child, Edward Alexander, on 24 February.[29] Benjamin scarcely had time to see the new baby before he was obliged to leave for the session of the legislature which opened in Quebec at the end of

February. The seat of government had been in Toronto for the previous four years, and by agreement was to be in Quebec for the next four. He was continuing to play an active role supporting the efforts of Macdonald's Liberal-Conservative coalition in the legislature, and his vote could not be missed.

As the entire civil service moved with the seat of government, Mannie, his oldest son was transferred with the post office and was now to live in Quebec for the next four years. For the moment, the expenses were more than Benjamin could handle. On 11 February 1860 he borrowed $200 on a mortgage of a small lot in town which he had bought from Rodney Moore, the printer, in 1851.[30]

Years previously, George Benjamin had become a successful politician in a place where there was no Jewish community, and had tried to blend in with the majority. More than 20 years earlier, Kingston's *British Whig* had attacked him as a "snarling hypocrite" — "the Saintly Belleville Jew" who was known to eat pork. Ten years later, Susanna Moodie had mocked him for disguising his Jewishness. Despite her efforts, Benjamin had been the first in Canada to have taken his seat in parliament as a known Jew. But could he have done it another way as a professing and participating Jew?

Selim Franklin had taken his seat as a member of the Legislative Assembly of Vancouver Island on 12 March 1860, without incident. He had been allowed to take his seat, even though he swore his oath of office as a Jew. He had made no secret of his religion and had been an active member of Victoria's Jewish community.[31] Canada had finally reached a stage where a Jew could hold a seat in an elected assembly, and still participate actively in Jewish communal life.

NOTES

[1] George Benjamin to Macdonald, 28 March 1858, Benjamin family papers, Toronto.

2 "North Hastings," *Hastings Chronicle*, 30 December 1857, p. 2, cols. 5-6.

3 *Intelligencer*, 4 December 1857, George Benjamin "To the Independent Electors of North Hastings" p. 1, col. 4; Philip Luke, "To the Free and Independent Electors of North Hastings," p. 2, col. 8 and p. 3, col. 1; "North Hastings," p. 2, col. 4; "A Globular," p. 2, col. 4.

4 *Intelligencer*, 18 December 1857.

5 "North Hastings," 30 December 1857, *loc. cit.*

6 "The Loretto Bill," *Intelligencer*, 11 December 1857, p. 2, cols. 5-6.

7 *Ibid.*

8 *Ibid.*

9 *Ibid.*

10 The process of officially separating church and state in Canada had begun by an act of the legislature only seven years earlier. The Act Respecting Rectories, 13 & 14 Vic., c. 175 (1851), had ended the established position of the Anglican Church in words that could only have cheered those searching out the land for a free and equal place to live. The Act provided as follows:

> "the free exercise and enjoyment of religious profession and worship, without discrimination or preference, so as the same be not made an excuse for acts of licentiousness, or a justification of practices inconsistent with the peace and safety of the Province, is by the constitution and laws of this Province allowed to all Her Majesty's subjects within the same."

11 "North Hastings," 30 December 1857, *loc. cit.*

12 D. G. Creighton, *John A. Macdonald: the young politician* (Toronto, MacMillan, 1956), pp. 259-60.

13 Macdonald to Benjamin, 12 January 1858, in *Papers of the prime ministers*, vol. II, pp. 6-7; Macdonald to Benjamin, 9 and 12 February 1858, in the possession of the Benjamin family, Toronto.

14 George Benjamin to Macdonald, 28 March 1858, *loc. cit.*

15 Emanuel Hyman Benjamin was appointed as a junior clerk, 4th class, in the Accountant's Office, Post Office Department, on 1 January 1857. On 1 July 1857 he was promoted to 3rd class clerk. *Report of the Postmaster General for the year ended 30 September 1857* (Toronto, John Lovell, 1858), p. 59. *See also* NAC, RG3, vol. 1029, p. 6.

16 Benjamin to Macdonald, 28 March 1858, *loc. cit.*

17 *Ibid.*

18 *See* chapter IX, note 27.

19 Robert Spence (1811-68) was appointed collector of customs at Toronto on Macdonald's recommendation shortly after his defeat in North Wentworth in December 1857, and held the post until his death. P. G. Cornell, "Robert Spence," *Dictionary of Canadian Biography*, vol. XI. Benjamin was quite incensed at the appointment, which involved an amendment to the Civil Service Act that allowed the position to be exempted from the procedures in the act. Benjamin wrote Macdonald on 28 March 1858, *loc. cit.*: "Instead of allowing the Member right and depriving the Government of Patronage, the whole power is in the hands of one or two Members of the Government, and only to be used for their friends in and about Toronto."

20 Benjamin to Macdonald, 28 March 1858, *loc. cit.*

21 "George C. Benjamin's Family Record, 1914," p. 5, mss. in the possession of the Benjamin family, Toronto.

22 George Benjamin to Macdonald, 28 March 1858, *loc. cit.*

23 Creighton, *op. cit.*, pp. 261-62.

24 *Ibid.*, pp. 261-72.

25 "Hastings Council," *Hastings Chronicle*, 26 January 1854, p. 2, col. 7; "Marmora Railway," 2 February 1859, p. 2, col. 2; "The Unkindest Cut of All," p. 2, col. 3.

26 *Intelligencer*, 1 February 1856, "County Council."

27 *Ibid.* The act to incorporate the Marmora and Belleville Railway Company was enacted in 1858 as 22 Vic., c. 121. The provisional directors included George Benjamin, Nathaniel S. Appelby, and Robert Read.

28 "Mr. Benjamin's Assertions," *Hastings Chronicle*, 27 March 1861, p. 3. The letter concluded, "The county would save many thousands of dollars annually if Benjamin and the whole crowd of such dishonest charlatans were driven from office, and compelled to live by honest labour instead of sponging on income cut of the public funds."

29 "George C. Benjamin's Family Record, 1914," p. 5.

30 Mortgage to Uriah West of lot 40, Edmund Murney's plan of lot 6, conc. 1, Thurlow Township, registered in the Hastings County Registry Office on 16 February 1860 as no. A 189.

31 C. E. Leonoff, *Pioneers, pedlars, and prayer shawls*, pp. 166-67; *Pioneer Jewish merchants of Vancouver Island and British Columbia* (a joint publication of the Jewish

Historical Society of British Columbia and the Jewish Western Bulletin, Vancouver, B. C., 1983), pp. 13-15. Selim Franklin (1814-83) was defeated at the general election of July 1863 but returned to the Legislative Assembly in a by-election early in 1864. He opposed the union of Vancouver Island with the mainland colony of British Columbia. When the union was consummated in 1866, he resigned his seat and returned to San Francisco. His older brother Lumley Franklin (1812-73) was elected second mayor of Victoria in 1866. *See also* David Rome, *The first two years: a record of Jewish pioneers on Canada's Pacific Coast, 1888-1860* (Montreal, H.M. Caiserman, 1942).

CHAPTER XI

The Promise Acknowledged

ॐ

"No one has better claims on the party
than yourself. You may be a *leetle* wanting in *Suaviter*.
However your ability is well known to us all."

John A. Macdonald to George Benjamin, 28 May 1861

BENJAMIN'S CAREER HAD REACHED A LOW POINT.

The session of the legislature that ended on 19 May 1860 had been difficult for George Benjamin. He had been obliged to travel back and forth between Belleville and Quebec several times during the session to look after the business of running Hastings County as well as to be on hand to support his party at votes in the legislature. He was 61 years old, overweight, and tired. His prospects of obtaining a position to retire upon seemed bleak. It had been two and a half years since the last election and John A. Macdonald's Liberal-Conservative coalition was still hanging on to power, though it lacked a majority. Macdonald had been unable to keep his promise and Benjamin's communication with his leader seemed to have deteriorated.

Just as Benjamin was leaving Quebec after the session had ended, Macdonald accosted him and accused him of having a conflict of interest in a tender Benjamin had approved. A few days after Benjamin arrived home, Macdonald wrote, telling Benjamin he had been mistaken and asking him to "accept my humble apology." Macdonald said he was "heartily sorry and ashamed and beg your forgiveness." "I hope after this," he concluded, "we will be as we were, and resume those terms of intimate and confidential intercourse that for so many years existed."[1] The letter was more than an apology. It was an invitation to Benjamin to resume their close relationship even though Macdonald could not for the time being keep his promise of finding him a permanent position.

Over the summer Benjamin and Macdonald wrote frequently. Through Macdonald, Benjamin was able to arrange for a number of appointments, including that of Nathaniel Appleby as Hastings' census commissioner. Appleby had used his casting vote to ensure Benjamin's election as warden in 1853 and, as incumbent warden in January 1859, had stood aside when Benjamin returned to Hastings County as warden in 1859.[2] Benjamin was less successful in having his son-in-law, Robert Newberry, appointed sheriff of Prince Edward County after the death of James McDonald had made that position available.[3] Instead, Macdonald recommended Henry J. Thorp, a Picton insurance agent, to be sheriff, "being recommended by almost every leading man in it."[4]

Macdonald and Benjamin had more correspondence about the big political event of the summer of 1860, the visit of the Prince of Wales. This was the first official visit of a member of the royal family to Canada. From Macdonald's point of view the visit was to be of great assistance in enhancing the fortunes of the Conservative party. Great celebrations were planned. The prince was to move westward aboard the steamer *Kingston* from Brockville to Kingston, then to Belleville, Cobourg, and Toronto. "If you have a court dress handy wear it," Macdonald told Benjamin. "If not, then black dress coat, vest and pants (as the Yankees call them) will do. White choker and gloves."[5]

The prince's visit worked out badly in both Kingston and Belleville. In both towns enthusiastic and unscheduled parades of Orangemen greeted the prince when he arrived. Parades of Orangemen were not legal in England at the time and the prince wished to avoid an incident at either location. The prince did not leave his steamer at either Kingston or Belleville, leaving the dignitaries at the scheduled receptions, including Macdonald and Benjamin, waiting at the dock, well dressed but disappointed.[6]

By the end of the year Benjamin's commitment to Macdonald remained, and he had decided to give Macdonald more time to keep his promise. At the municipal elections in January 1861, Benjamin was re-elected to the Hungerford Township Council, selected as its reeve, and again re-elected as warden of Hastings County.[7]

As he had the previous year, Benjamin went off to Quebec for the opening of the 1861 session of the legislature on 16 March, splitting his time between municipal and provincial politics. Six days after the session started, parliament adjourned for a ten-day Easter recess. Along with other members, Benjamin supported the recess. The *Hastings Chronicle*, in the service of its Orange and Protestant readership, regarded the vote for the long recess as a concession to the demands of the French Catholics of Quebec and recalled that in 1858 when parliament sat in Toronto, it had taken only a one-day adjournment over the Easter holiday. The *Hastings Chronicle* attacked Benjamin personally for his support of the decision and, with a general election in the offing, reminded the electorate of Benjamin's Jewish background. After referring to Benjamin as "the independent, honest, Protestant member for North Hastings," the *Hastings Chronicle* continued: "we would beg to ask the ex-Grand Master if he remembers the year of the Christian era 1858, (we really don't remember the Jewish Chronology or we would ask him in his native language)."[8]

When the session of the legislature ended on 18 May, it was obvious that there was to be a general election. Macdonald's coalition had hung on to power for three and a half years with the exception of the two day "double shuffle," when George Brown's Grits had formed the government in the summer of 1858. Macdonald pressed Benjamin to run again. Benjamin, taking a new tack, wanted to be in Macdonald's cabinet before the election. "No one has better claims on the party than yourself." Macdonald replied. "You may be a *leetle* wanting in *Suaviter*. However your ability is well known to us all. We will *not* re-construct before the elections." Macdonald's advice was that Benjamin should stay in politics until after the election and then they could see about getting him a position.[9] "As your friend however," said Macdonald, "if we get a majority so as to carry a Bill next Session, I would advise you to go *in* for the permanent office about printing, rather than risk the peril of a turn out every five minutes."[10]

When the election was called in June, Benjamin once again declared himself a candidate in Hastings North. His opponent, Thomas Campbell Wallbridge, was the brother of the member for Hastings South, Lewis Wallbridge.[11] The major issue in the 1861 election was "Rep by Pop" — the term of the day used to express the phrase "representation by population." Census figures released just before the election confirmed that the population of Canada West had grown to such a degree that it now greatly exceeded the population of Canada East.[12] The Act of Union of 1840, which had united Upper and Lower Canada into the new Province of Canada, had created equality of the regions by allowing each area an equal number of seats. But now that the English-speaking population of Canada West was greater than that of French-speaking Canada East, George Brown and his Grit Liberals wanted a basis of representation that would acknowledge Canada West's larger population, by giving it more seats than Canada East.

Macdonald, whose main support in parliament came from Canada East, was officially against "Rep by Pop."[13] George Benjamin, who supported Macdonald but needed the support of his own electorate, who were predominantly Orange and anti-French, had a fine line to toe. During the last session of parliament he had actually made a speech endorsing "Rep by Pop."[14] During the election campaign, Macdonald told Benjamin he could continue to support "Rep by Pop" even if his party opposed it. "Go for Rep by Pop as strongly if [sic] you like, but do *not* say that it must be granted if a majority of U.C. members say so. Such a proposition ... in fact affirms that the House of Assembly is to be governed by a minority." And, Macdonald added, "say that the principle is so just and equitable that it must prevail and you have no doubt it will eventually carry."[15] On the other hand, Macdonald had some advice for Benjamin about keeping the support of the Catholics, not just in his riding but across Canada. "As you are situated *do not put yourself in opposition to the French.* You are popular with them and not overpopular with the U.C. members of the last House. The French are your Sheet anchor. *Verbum Sap.*"[16]

When the votes were counted in Hastings North at the end of July, Benjamin was elected — his victory once again being based on support by both Protestant and Catholic electors. The support by the Protestants was to be expected. Benjamin, of course, had been a grand master of the Orange lodge and had introduced a bill into parliament to incorporate the Orange society. The support by the Catholics was harder to explain, although the *Hastings Chronicle* came close to the mark: "If they have voted for him hitherto," it said of the Catholics, "it was not on account of the love they bore towards him as a man, but because he was the most acceptable, politically, to them, of the candidates who came forward at the respective Elections. ... It was not because they thought him more economical than others as regards the pecuniary offices of this great and growing Province; but that no other man willing (at least theoretically) to extend to them their rights and privileges as a religious body presented himself for their suffrages."[17]

Despite the negative remarks it had previously printed about Benjamin's Jewish roots, the *Hastings Chronicle* seemed to understand his underlying motivation. He had been the only one of the candidates to sympathize with aspirations of the Catholics to exercise civil and political rights equally with other religious groups.

Throughout Canada, Macdonald's candidates fared better than in the previous election, but they did not have a comfortable majority. John Sandfield Macdonald had surprised everyone by having a large group of his Liberal supporters elected, enough to rival George Brown's Grit Liberal group. Sandfield had run on the platform of a "double majority," a principle whereby government should not continue against the parliamentary wishes of a majority from either Canada East or Canada West.

Macdonald's words must have echoed in Benjamin's ears. His government seemed "firmly in the saddle." He had "a majority so as to carry a Bill." Now, Benjamin had every right to expect the promise to be kept.

NOTES

1 John A. Macdonald to George Benjamin, 30 May 1860, Benjamin family papers, *loc. cit.* The letter opened: "Accept my humble apology for having asserted or insinuated that you were personally or pecuniarily interested in [making?] Lovell's Tender a success. This had been insinuated to *me*, but I did not for a moment believe it."

2 NAC, Macdonald to Benjamin, 28 June 1860; Benjamin family papers, Macdonald to Benjamin, 11, 26 July 1860.

3 *Ibid.*, Robert Newberry married the Benjamins' oldest daughter, Esther Eliza, at St Thomas' Church in Belleville on 6 August 1856. St Thomas' records, register no. 7-B-4 (1852-71), p. 113; *Intelligencer*, 8 August 1856, p. 3, col. 2.

4 Macdonald to Benjamin, 26 July 1860, *loc. cit.*

5 NAC, Macdonald to Benjamin, 2 July, 4 August 1860.

6 Creighton, *op. cit.*, pp. 301-3 as to Kingston; Mika, *op. cit.*, pp. 40-41 as to Belleville.

7 Victoria District *Records and Proceedings*, vol. II, p. 1100.

8 "Six Days Work, Sixteen Days Pay!," *Hastings Chronicle*, 27 March 1861, p. 3.

9 NAC, Macdonald to Benjamin, 28 May 1861.

10 *Ibid.* According to Mackenzie Bowell, Benjamin, as member of the printing committee of the legislature, affected "a saving of $500,000 in one parliament." "George Benjamin, Esq.," *loc. cit.*

11 Lewis Wallbridge (1816-87) was a lawyer and Reform politician. He replaced Billa Flint as member of the legislature in 1857 for Hastings South, and held the seat until 1867.

12 Creighton, *op. cit.*, p. 308. The population of Canada West exceeded the population of Canada East by 285,000, according to the 1861 census.

13 *Ibid.*, pp. 326-28.

14 *Ibid.*, p. 308.

15 NAC, Macdonald to Benjamin, 4 June 1861.

16 *Ibid.*, *verbum sap*: enough said; a word to the wise.

17 *Hastings Chronicle*, 7 August 1861, "For the Hastings Chronicle."

CHAPTER XII

Promises, Promises

ﮊ

"In no one instance have I failed you, but your
promises to me, as well for the interests of others, as
myself, remain to be fulfilled. I do not say what I now write to
threaten or in anger, but it does appear to me that you think ...
that I must depend on you for that retiring position; but do
not mistake me, rather than submit to this I would
break stones on the street for a living."

George Benjamin to John A. Macdonald, Quebec,
13 August 1861

NOW THAT THE GENERAL ELECTION OF JUNE 1861 WAS OVER, BENJAMIN'S EFFORTS
turned towards finding a government appointment to some office. An
unexpected opportunity presented itself just before the election ended.
On 19 July, William Hutton the secretary of the Bureau of Agriculture,
had died in Quebec City. Benjamin had known Hutton well when he
served as warden of Victoria District. After Hutton's position as county
school superintendent had been terminated by the County of Hastings
in 1850, Hutton had written a prize essay on agriculture and had become
an employee of the government. As secretary of the Bureau of Agriculture
he became, in effect, the senior civil servant in what would later be known
as the Department of Agriculture.[1]

Benjamin went to Quebec as soon as the election was over to see what
he could do about getting appointed to Hutton's job.[2] Benjamin met
Macdonald and asked him point blank. Macdonald was non-committal.
Benjamin pressed the point, but received no reply. Benjamin closed off,
"well I think I have said everything and know how matters stand. I go off

tomorrow and may not see you again." He held out his hand and added "so good bye." Macdonald did not want the matter to drop. "Oh I will be in office tomorrow," he said, "look in before you go, if anything occurs to you."[3]

When Benjamin returned to his room, he received a note from Macdonald, confirming the invitation. The note said Benjamin had been talking to everyone about him, that good-natured friends of both of them took care to exaggerate Benjamin's complimentary remarks when reporting to Macdonald — as if Benjamin was voicing critical opinions about Macdonald out of earshot.[4] Benjamin had to speak to Macdonald again. Macdonald's note signalled a serious change in their relations and Benjamin did not understand it. Immediately, he sent Macdonald a note saying he would come by Macdonald's office at 11:30 the next morning, 13 August, the day Benjamin had arranged to return by rail to Belleville. He got to Macdonald's office that morning. He waited more than two hours. Macdonald did not appear.[5]

Benjamin felt hurt and frustrated. Promises had been made to him by Macdonald and not kept. Matters had been placed before Macdonald on behalf of Benjamin's constituents, and ignored. Benjamin had submitted quietly to delays, while others who were fickle in their support of the government, were given immediate results. Benjamin left to go.[6]

On the way to the train, he ran into William Powell,[7] a supporter of Macdonald in parliament since 1854, but never a cabinet minister. Almost as soon as the general election of 1861 was over, Powell had started talking much too publicly about Macdonald. The word was that he and other discontented Conservatives were going to desert the ministry.[8]

Powell asked Benjamin if he had any news. Benjamin replied that he had none, and according to Benjamin's report to Macdonald on 13 August, the conversation developed in the following words:

"Mr. Benjamin," said Powell, "do you know that you and I will never be advanced in our political position while John A. is at the head of affairs?"

"It is possible," answered Benjamin. "Mr. Macdonald is quite aware of my opinions upon the matter."

Powell continued: "Do you know that Macdonald has been heard to say that he hated both you and I to that degree that he could not see us before him?"

Benjamin was crushed. "I was not aware that he had said so," said Benjamin. "I cannot think it."

Powell assured him that it was true and that he was going to swear out a statutory declaration to prove it.

Benjamin returned to his room and drafted a long letter to Macdonald. He told him he could wait no longer to see him, since Macdonald had not kept his appointment and Benjamin had to return home. He told Macdonald what Powell had said. He wrote: "I cannot conceive that I have done aught to render me so frightfully obnoxious to you. Of course I have no right to question your likes and dislikes, but after a political itinerary of twenty years, during which I can honestly say I have made my own position a Secondary consideration to yours in all our intercourse, I did not want to be told such a tale by Mr. Powell. I saw nothing that could place my conduct on a par with his, and I must confess I did feel hurt." Benjamin continued: "In no one instance have I failed you, but your promises to me, as well for the interests of others, as myself, remain to be fulfilled. I do not say what I now write to threaten or in anger, but it does appear to me that you think that from the fact of your Knowing that as I grow older and in years I need to retire and need something to retire upon, and you know that I am so perfectly at variance with other parties, that I must depend on you for that retiring position; but do not mistake me, rather than submit to this I would break stones on the street for a living." He concluded: "I do not desire in this letter to renew any former applications, as it remains with you Sir to determine whether our intercourse is to continue on its old foundation, or whether entirely new relations are to be called into existence."[9] And he returned home on the train.

Benjamin's opponents, who had previously suspected that "it may be probable" that he had seen "a Government appointment to some office on the horizon,"[10] now knew for a fact that Benjamin wanted an appointment. The *Hastings Chronicle* was merciless in its exposé of Benjamin as office seeker. Referring to him as "the 'fat boy' of the North," the editorial noted that "Everybody who knows anything of Mr. Benjamin, knows he has been dangling after every office that has been the gift of the Government for the last five years." The editorial remarked at his haste in going to Quebec so soon after Hutton had died, and compared him to a shark following a ship for days "waiting for the corpse of the dying man to be cast overboard."[11]

All this must have been quite embarrassing for Benjamin, but Macdonald was in no hurry to make an appointment to fill Hutton's office. When Benjamin wrote Macdonald in September about another matter, Macdonald took the opportunity to reply that "you are as hot-headed as anyone."[12] Several weeks went by without any further word. Finally, on 19 October, Macdonald composed a reply.[13] He apologized to Benjamin for not keeping the appointment at his office in Quebec in August. He had been detained until two at his house by a crowd of visitors, and when he got to his office he found Benjamin had just left.[14] At the time, he had not realized that Benjamin felt there was anything important left to discuss. Macdonald assured him of prompt action on all the constituency matters Benjamin had raised. He told him not to worry about the doings of the "Ornamental Member" — an allusion to William Powell, who may have looked like a supporter in form, but whose words were of no moment.

There was no good news about finding a position for Benjamin. Filling up Hutton's office was not Macdonald's decision but that of the entire Cabinet or Executive Council. "Whenever the Council agree to fill up Hutton's office," he said, "I will do what I can to secure it for you, but I can give you no assurance that I will succeed." Macdonald explained that "the Head of the Department in which the vacancy occurs has the right to decide."

This was the kiss of death for Benjamin's hopes. The head of the department, the minister of agriculture, was none other than John Ross, whom Benjamin had known well in Belleville. Ross had been Robert Baldwin's lieutenant in the violent 1841 Hastings election and had often confronted Benjamin as a political opponent. After his appointment to the Legislative Council, Ross, though a Reformer, had drifted over to support Macdonald's Liberal-Conservative coalition and had been appointed minister of agriculture in 1858.[15] There was still too much personal animus between Ross and Benjamin to give him any hope that Ross would agree to his appointment. "If I cannot get that office for you," Macdonald concluded, "I must get some other."[16]

So there matters stood. It was almost four years since Macdonald had promised Benjamin "an appointment to retire upon that would please my friends and sustain my position."[17] While the promise was to have been kept before the end of that session, four sessions had passed, and now another election, and still no result. Macdonald still had no clear cut majority in the house and could not be held to account.

Benjamin had few options left. He was now 62 years old. All he could do was wait.

George Benjamin, MPP, photograph c. 1859.

NOTES

1 W. B. Turner, "William Hutton," *loc. cit.*

2 "Will He Get an Office?," *Hastings Chronicle*, 7 August 1861.

3 NAC, Macdonald to Benjamin, 19 October 1861.

4 Benjamin to Macdonald, Quebec, 13 August 1861, copy, Benjamin family papers.

5 Macdonald to Benjamin, 19 October 1861, *loc. cit.*

6 Benjamin to Macdonald, 13 August 1861, *loc. cit.*

7 William Frederick Powell (1826-1887/95) was born in Perth and moved to Bytown (Ottawa) by 1847. After serving as reeve of Bytown, he represented Carleton in the parliament of the Province of Canada from 1854 to 1867.

8 Robert Spence wrote to Macdonald in September 1861 that "William F. Powell has been in Toronto abusing their Ministry and holding conferences with J. H. Cameron." D. G. Creighton, *John A. Macdonald: the young politician* (Toronto, Macmillan, 1856), p. 137.

9 Benjamin to Macdonald, 13 August 1861, *loc. cit.*

10 "For the Hastings Chronicle," 7 August 1861.

11 "Will He Get an Office?," *loc. cit.*

12 Macdonald to Benjamin, 11 September 1861, Benjamin family papers.

13 Macdonald to Benjamin, 19 October 1861, *loc. cit.*

14 The irony of this remark would not have been lost on Benjamin, who made a point of not pressing Macdonald at home, only at the office. He had written Macdonald on 13 August: "Few public men take up less of your time than I do, I have never except upon special solicitation troubled you at your own dwelling."

15 Paul Cornell, "John Ross," *loc. cit.*

16 Macdonald to Benjamin, 14 October 1861, *loc. cit.*

17 Benjamin to Macdonald, 28 March 1858, *loc. cit.*

CHAPTER XIII

The Price of Loyalty

ຂ຺

"A man may waste all his means for his party
and be led on by promises, made only to be broken, as
they knew poor father would not desert them."

Emanuel Hyman Benjamin to his uncle Abraham Cohen
in Australia, 30 September 1864

FRIDAY, 14 MARCH 1862, THE SHIRE HALL, BELLEVILLE. DURING THE THIRD session of Hastings County Council for the year, a special meeting of council was called "to consider a communication from the Attorney General's office respecting the present position of the Council."[1] The meeting had been called by George Benjamin as warden,[2] as well as by Nathaniel S. Appleby as warden.[3] Confusion reigned.

For Benjamin it was the beginning of the end. He had been unanimously re-elected as warden on 28 January at the first session of council.[4] Three weeks before that he had been re-elected to the Hungerford Township Council, in ward one, and had been again selected as reeve. All that was usual enough.[5] But his opponent in ward one of Hungerford, a man named Windsor W. Jones, had contested Benjamin's election in court, claiming that the township clerk, in making out the voters' list, had omitted the names of many of the voters of the ward.[6] Within a day after Benjamin's election as warden, the court declared Benjamin's return as a Hungerford councillor to be void, and ordered a new election to be held the following month.[7] The court did not find that Benjamin had any part in the omission of names from the voters' list, nor that the clerk had done anything wrong. The Toronto *Globe* heralded Benjamin's voided election as proof of his waning popularity and suggested[8] that "it follows that his election as warden will be set aside."[9] Benjamin's opponents were jubilant: Billa Flint flew a large banner from his store proclaiming the words "Benjamin Beaten."[10]

Benjamin lost when he faced Jones in the by-election in mid February. Prior to the election he was offered another ward in the township but refused it on the ground that if not elected for ward one, he should not be on council at all.[11] Jones, victorious in ward one and later selected reeve of Hungerford by the other councillors, presented his credentials and took his seat at the second meeting of county council on 25 February 1862. Benjamin had not been invited. There was a great deal of confusion about whether Benjamin was still the warden.

The county solicitor, John Bell, had given his opinion that Benjamin was warden until unseated. He had been legally elected reeve of Hungerford and was properly qualified when unanimously chosen as warden. The court had unseated him as a councillor of Hungerford, but not as warden of Hastings. What is more, no one could challenge the validity of Benjamin's election as warden since no one had voted against him when he was unanimously chosen. The only way to remove Benjamin legally was to ask him to resign.[12] Billa Flint, reeve of Elzevir Township, did not agree. Though he was not a lawyer, he was relying on the opinion of his lawyer, Lewis Wallbridge, the Liberal member of the assembly for Hastings South, to the effect that the meeting was legally called by the county clerk and that a new warden would be elected by the members present. Other members of the county council felt that Flint was trying to lead them "into a slough hole" and that the whole proceedings were "child's play."[13]

Finally, Flint persuaded the members of council to hold a new election for warden, knowing that it might not be a valid election, but seeing it as the only means of getting on with the county's business. As he said, "it was evident that the lawyers could not settle it, and it was only the Judges that could ... . It was better to proceed, and if wrong, petition Parliament to set them right."[14] A. F. Wood, reeve of Madoc Township, and Nathaniel S. Appleby, reeve of Tyendinaga Township, were both nominated. The result was a tie — six votes each — and Appleby as reeve of the municipality with the largest number of electors on the assessment roll was given the casting vote. Appleby voted for himself saying he was obliged to do so "in justice to those who had supported him." He was then sworn in as warden.

Immediately after the meeting, Appleby told Benjamin what had happened. Benjamin knew he was still warden. He also knew he had to resign. He had expected to be called to the meeting and would have resigned then. But no one had asked him to come. He heard of the confusion about legal opinions and wrote to the attorney general's office for an opinion himself.

By the end of the first week in March, the attorney general's opinion, signed by Hewitt Bernard, the chief legal officer, and incidentally later the brother-in-law of John A. Macdonald, was received.[15] It confirmed the county solicitor's opinion that Benjamin was warden until he resigned.[16] Benjamin at once called a meeting for 10 March. At the request of the county clerk, Appleby also sent out notices of the meeting "as probably some of the members will not attend on Mr. Benjamin's summons and it will be necessary to have a full meeting in order that the trouble may be finally settled."[17]

In the end, everyone came to the meeting. There was some discussion about the attorney general's opinion. Someone, undoubtedly Flint, suggested that the opinion would only be binding on the county council if signed by the attorney general himself — John A. Macdonald — and not by his deputy, Bernard. But everyone else seemed to accept the opinion and Benjamin was asked to speak. It was his farewell speech to county politics. He reminded his listeners that during his long term of office the county had increased in population and wealth, that 90 bridges and 150 miles of roads had been built without increasing taxes by more than the level required by inflation and that the credit of the county had been sustained.[18]

Then he resigned and the councillors voted what Bowell later referred to as "a very flattering Resolution: ... expressive of regret on his retirement from Municipal life."[19] The resolution was not unanimous. Billa Flint voted against it as did Windsor W. Jones, the newly elected reeve of

Hungerford Township. Flint said he would have voted for the resolution if it had been limited to thanking Benjamin for his job as warden and had not mentioned his resigning. He did accept the opinion that Benjamin was still warden until he resigned.[20] Before the meeting ended, the councillors had another vote to select a warden. Appleby was elected, 14 votes to 2 — Flint and Jones dissenting.[21]

Benjamin left for Quebec almost immediately after the county council meetings. The new session of the legislature was to open on 20 March, and with the narrowness of Macdonald's majority, every vote would count. Events in the legislature took a surprising turn almost from the outset. At the opening of the legislature, Macdonald had promised a free vote on "Rep by Pop." The opposition had surprised him by making the issue a question of confidence in the government and moving that the government should be defeated on that issue. Most of the members for Canada West had surprised Macdonald even more when, on 1 April 1862, 43 voted in favour of the motion for "Rep by Pop" and only 16 against. Macdonald's government was saved only by the bulk of the votes of the French Canadian members from Canada East.[22]

George Benjamin had been among those voting for "Rep by Pop." He had promised it to his constituents in the last election and had been encouraged by Macdonald himself. Now he found himself as spokesman for a group that Macdonald saw as having defected from party policy and voted against the government on a matter of confidence. The meeting of the "defectors" on 2 April unanimously chose Benjamin to make peace with Macdonald. Benjamin, the spokesman, assured Macdonald that those who had voted for "Rep by Pop" believed the government was quite safe and "it was not their intention to vote a want of confidence." "I can only say," Benjamin concluded, "I never attended a more cordial meeting of friends, nor one where the feeling was more united in favour of yourself as their leader, and in confidence in your ability to conduct the affairs of the country."[23]

Macdonald's government lasted only six more weeks. It had been continuously in power for almost ten years, with the exception of the "double shuffle" period in 1858. Now, on 2 May, after Macdonald had introduced the Militia Bill, the consensus of English and French that had allowed him to hold power fell apart. The American Civil War had started a year earlier. Britain as well as its Canadian ministers were concerned with the power of the great army of the United States. Macdonald's Militia Bill was to provide for the training of 30,000 men who would be volunteers if possible, but conscripts if necessary. The bill was debated for several days amid growing public concern. Finally, on 20 May, a small group of French Canadian votes changed sides and the Conservatives were defeated by a vote of 61 to 54.[24]

Then a remarkable thing happened. On 21 May 1862 Governor General Lord Monck called upon John Sandfield Macdonald to form a government. Sandfield, although he was leader of only one group of Liberals, associated himself with L.-V. Sicotte, the leader of a larger group of French Canadians from Canada East, and satisfied himself that he would have majority support. George Benjamin had long been an opponent of John Sandfield Macdonald.[25] He had been in parliament for many years as a supporter of John A. Macdonald's Conservatives. He had not been given an office to retire upon or a cabinet position, and now, frankly, it was out of John A. Macdonald's power to help him any more. Benjamin was forceful, able, and well liked, particularly by the French-speaking members. He had balanced the books as warden of Hastings County. He was 63 years old.

On the same day, 21 May 1862, John Sandfield Macdonald asked Benjamin to be his minister of finance. Benjamin's acceptance of Sandfield's offer would have made him the first Jewish cabinet minister in Canada, 107 years before a Jew actually became a member of a Canadian cabinet.[26] According to Benjamin's son Mannie, "the office was kept open three days for his answer, yet he would not leave his party even after they had broken their promises. Poor father," he continued, "preferred to go to his grave poor and without a stain on his name than with riches and have it said he was a traitor."[27] On 24 May 1862 William Pearce Howland was appointed as the new minister of finance.[28]

Benjamin finished out the session, which ended on 9 June. He kept doing his job as a member of the assembly. He introduced the first Petty Trespass Bill into the legislature and it was passed into law.[29] He was even, for a time, inclined to support Sandfield's government.[30] But it was all

John Sandfield Macdonald, 1863.

over. Benjamin could never run for parliament again. He had few resources. The property he owned was all encumbered. He told Mackenzie Bowell he was finished but that he would help Bowell win Hastings North once a new election was called. Likely he even made an arrangement with Bowell to take over the *Intelligencer* again when Bowell won.

There was one last score to settle before he left parliament. In 1856 John Wedderburn Dunbar Moodie, the sheriff of Hastings and husband of Susanna Moodie, had made the mistake of selling the office of deputy sheriff in his department, rather than appointing a deputy based on his ability. Sheriff Moodie had received £300 for appointing the new deputy to office.[31] It was a clear-cut error, much more serious than the error of the registry clerk that had cost Benjamin his job as registrar in 1854. Court proceedings for Moodie's removal were started as soon as his error became known, but the proceedings dragged on. Moodie, in need of the job as a livelihood, would not resign — even though a stroke in 1861 left him partly paralyzed. Benjamin had done his part to have the proceedings expedited but had been unsuccessful.[32] By October 1861 Benjamin said that the question of Moodie's dismissal as sheriff was "the most important" of the matters he had placed before Macdonald's government.[33] Finally, in January 1863, Moodie resigned, two months before a court actually convicted him, on a finding that he had transgressed unintentionally.[34]

Susanna Moodie and her husband, J. W. Dunbar Moodie,
in front of their cottage on Bridge Street, Belleville, c. 1860.

Immediately after the 1863 session of the legislature ended on 12 May, a new election was called. Just as Benjamin was ready to announce his retirement, he got another letter from his leader. Macdonald wanted him to run again. There would be no money from the party to help in the campaign, and Macdonald was no longer promising to give him any position to retire upon. "It appears to me," the letter concluded, "that you should have no difficulty in getting money from your Belleville friends as a discount on your Salary as Speaker — It is quite certain that you will be Elected Speaker, if elected Member. So that it is worth while to invest a considerable sum of money in getting your Seat."[35]

Macdonald's words seemed to mean that Benjamin was now to rely on the other parties to help him secure sufficient income, by supporting him as speaker. He would waste no more time. "After mature deliberation," he wrote to the public through the columns of the *Intelligencer* on 29 May, "I have made up my mind not to offer for the North Riding of the County of Hastings at the coming election."[36] The *Montreal Gazette* took notice. "His absence from Parliament will be noticed and felt," said its editorial. "He was one of the oldest and ablest of its members, and his experience is only equalled by his intimate acquaintance with our political affairs and untiring application. Amid the charges of corruption which have so recklessly bandied in the interest of faction, it is notable that Mr. Benjamin, during his long career, has never made any personal gain. On the contrary, his public services have been at the cost of his private interests."[37]

On 30 May 1863, at O'Dell's Tavern, Mackenzie Bowell was selected as candidate in Hastings North for the Conservatives and Thomas Campbell Wallbridge, who had lost against Benjamin in the 1861 election, was selected for the Liberals.[38] The campaign was all over for Benjamin within a week. He had promised to help Bowell and went out to the back areas of the riding to make speeches. As his family in England heard it, Benjamin "had been addressing an assemblage *outdoors* during a continuous rain and the damp and cold had struck into him."[39] He fell severely ill and returned home. He was bedridden for the rest of the campaign and was at home when he got the news of Bowell's loss to Wallbridge. He thought he was getting better over the summer, but when autumn came his condition was worse.

By December 1863 the lower part of his body and his limbs became paralyzed and he was in great pain. He summoned his son Emanuel in Quebec to come and see him, fearing the worst. Emanuel, giving "all the particulars," reported to his uncle Abraham on 13 December. "I find him very much changed as his sufferings have been something more than ordinary," he wrote. "He was attended for inflammation of the lung &

Mackenzie Bowell, c. 1864, in militia uniform.

kidneys but it now turns out that he should have been treated for *rheumatic neuralgia*. This you will readily see must have allowed the latter complaint to take a much firmer grasp that [*sic*] if it had been treated for it in the first place. He has lost in flesh during his sickness more than Eighty pounds in weight. This can do no harm, but at the same time it has reduced his strength very materially." "What also retards father's recovery," he continued, "is the sudden change from an active life to one that does not require even the ordinary matters of business to excite and keep his mind actively employed. Few men of his weight led such an active life or could stand the same amount of bodily fatigue as my father."[40] The worst was yet to come.

NOTES

1 "Notice," Belleville Public Library, Hastings County Historical Society Collection, no. 748-1. *See also Intelligencer,* "County Council," 14 March 1862.

2 *Intelligencer,* "County Council," 21 March 1862, p. 2, col. 5.

3 Victoria District/Hastings County Council *Records and Proceedings,* vol. III (1861-1871), p. 76, in the possession of the clerk, County of Hastings, Belleville.

4 *Ibid.,* p. 67.

5 *Intelligencer,* "Municipal Elections," 10 January 1862.

6 *Intelligencer,* "Mr. Benjamin's Election in Hungerford," 7 February 1862. As to Windsor W. Jones *see Intelligencer,* 21 February 1862, "Ward Election in Hungerford," and Hastings County Council minutes, *loc. cit.,* 25 February 1862.

7 *Ibid.*

8 *Ibid.*

9 *Globe,* "Wardens for 1862," 31 January 1862, p. 2, col. 5.

10 *Intelligencer,* 7 February 1862, *op. cit.*

11 *Intelligencer,* "Ward Election in Hungerford," 21 February 1862.

12 *Intelligencer* "County Council," 25 February 1862.

13 *Ibid.*

14 *Ibid.*

15 P. B. Waite, "Hewitt Bernard," *Dictionary of Canadian Biography,* vol. XII.

16 *Intelligencer,* "County Council," 21 March 1862, p. 2, cols. 4-7.

17 "Notice," *loc. cit.*

18 *Intelligencer,* 21 March 1862, *loc. cit.*

19 [Bowell], "George Benjamin, Esq."

20 *Intelligencer,* 21 March 1862, *loc. cit. See also* Hastings County Council minutes, *loc. cit.,* 14 March 1862, p. 77.

21 *Ibid.,* p. 79.

22 Creighton, *op. cit.,* pp. 327-66.

23 *Ibid.,* p. 328.

[24] *Ibid.*, pp. 329-33.

[25] A year later Benjamin was to write to an associate that Sandfield "is a man of no principle, a man of no political opinion, one who has not understanding enough to be classed as a tenth rate statesman." Benjamin to Isaac Buchanan, 10 August 1863, NAC, MG24, D 16, pp. 1632-43.

[26] On 20 October 1969 Herbert Gray, who had been member of parliament for Essex West since 1962, was sworn in as minister without portfolio in the government led by Pierre Elliot Trudeau, becoming the first Canadian federal cabinet minister of the Jewish faith. As cabinet ministers normally took their oaths on a copy of the New Testament, which was thereupon presented to them, Gray provided a Hebrew Bible for the ceremony. At this ceremony and at subsequent ceremonies when he was sworn in to other cabinet portfolios, Gray wore the traditional skull cap or *kippah*. David A. Croll had become the first cabinet minister of the Jewish faith in a Canadian provincial government when he was sworn into the Ontario government led by Mitchell Hepburn in 1933, as minister of municipal affairs, with two other portfolios.

[27] Emanuel Hyman Benjamin to Abraham Cohen, 30 September 1864, Abraham Cohen family papers.

[28] Bruce W. Hodgins, *John Sandfield Macdonald 1812-1872* (Toronto, University of Toronto Press, 1971); "John Sandfield Macdonald," *Dictionary of Canadian Biography*, vol. X.

[29] *Intelligencer*, 4 July 1862, p. 1.

[30] George Benjamin to Isaac Buchanan, 10 August 1863, *loc. cit.*

[31] Macdonald to Benjamin, 28 May 1861, in *The letters of Sir John A. Macdonald, 1858-1861*, *op. cit.*, p. 331, n. 1.

[32] Macdonald to Benjamin, 28 March 1861, *loc. cit.* Macdonald to Benjamin 25 January 1862, Benjamin family papers.

[33] Benjamin to Macdonald, 13 August 1861, *loc. cit.*

[34] Carl Ballstadt, "John Wedderburn Dunbar Moodie," *Dictionary of Canadian Biography*, vol. IX.

[35] Macdonald to Benjamin, 21 May 1863, Benjamin family papers.

[36] *Intelligencer*, 29 May 1863.

[37] *Intelligencer*, 5 June 1863, p. 2, quoting the *Montreal Gazette*.

[38] *Intelligencer*, "North Riding of Hastings," 5 June 1863, p. 2.

[39] Emphasis in original. Nathan Cohen, Brighton, to Abraham Cohen, Sydney, 19 October 1864, Abraham Cohen family papers. *See also* Emanuel Hyman Benjamin to Isaac Buchanan, 7 November 1864, NAC, MG24, D 16, pp. 1623-31.

[40] Emanuel H. Benjamin, Belleville, to Abraham Cohen, Sydney, 13 December 1863, Abraham Cohen family papers.

CHAPTER XIV

The Legacy

"I regret to say I still continue to
be an invalid and confined to my Room.
You were kind enough on a former occasion to
address me, in terms of kindness, so much so, I am
induced to ask a favor at your hands. I believe you have
several Commercial Establishments in Canada. I have a son
a lad of about 18 who has just left school here, who I am
desirous of getting out into the world. I do not care about his
obtaining any amount of pay at present beyond what will clothe
and feed him, and must trust to his industry and perseverance to
push himself forward. Can you give such a lad employment. He
is willing to work and learn, and has some idea of men and
business. Do excuse me, if you think I have taken a liberty, but
my anxiety would not let me rest, until I had written this. I
expected to have obtained a place for him in a Bank, but failed,
and in consequence of the Bank curtailing instead of increasing.
Unable from my severe illness to attend to business since my
confinement I am compelled to seek to put my sons out
with as little delay as possible. I will say no more as I
do not wish to write in praise of my own child."

George Benjamin to Isaac Buchanan, 18 December 1863

JUST AS HE STARTED LAPSING, GEORGE BENJAMIN AWOKE TO THE REALIZATION
that his family had not yet been provided for. His oldest, Mannie, had a
good position with the post office. Ettie had been married to Robert
Newberry since 1856, but Newberry's employment prospects needed
assistance. Lewis Nathan had just finished law school at McGill in
Montreal. His third son, Ellis Ralph, had a job with the Bank of Upper

Canada. His fourth son, Harry Ansell, "a lad of about 18,"[1] had just finished school and had no prospects. There were seven more children at home with Isabella and her mother. There was no income beyond what the oldest boys could send them; all their assets were encumbered.

By a superhuman effort, Benjamin spent his last months getting organized. His letter to Isaac Buchanan resulted in Harry getting a temporary job as clerk in the legislature. He managed to get Lewis Nathan placed with the Montreal law firm owned by his former colleague in parliament, John Joseph Caldwell Abbott. He got Robert appointed as collector of inland revenue for Hastings County. He had begged, he had pleaded, he had called in his debts.[2] There were other arrangements too. His son George Lipman Benjamin, who had drowned in 1848, had not been baptized and was not buried in St Thomas' churchyard, as was his son Charles Angus. On 8 January 1864 George Benjamin and his wife, Isabella, were both baptized by John Grier, rector of St Thomas' Church.[3] The ceremony likely took place at home. Benjamin was confined to his room. The witnesses were their daughters Ettie and Tilly.

Isaac Buchanan (1810-83).

As time passed, he wrote letters and said goodbye in his own way. In May he wrote his brother Abraham in Australia, telling him, "I wrote this on the flat of my back," and that "when I tell you I have lost the use of my legs for the last four months you will I am sure conclude that there is something more than fancy about my illness." He said that a person should always find time to write to absent relatives and that he would be sending a gift of a copy of the family's seal to Australia. He explained the symbolism of the family crest and said that "we were the lineal offspring from the first High Priest on record, Aaron. Our name was not simply Cohen but Hacohen."[4]

Benjamin's intellect was still very much alive. In the midst of it all, he conceived of a desperate scheme to earn some capital for his family. The legislature still met at Quebec but the seat of government was to move to Ottawa as soon as the new Parliament Buildings were ready. Up to now, Benjamin had obtained no position from the government. A ministry led by John A. Macdonald had once again taken control of the government, about three months earlier. If he could use whatever influence he had left, he might be able to get the contract to move parliament from Quebec to its new home in Ottawa. If the contract price for the move was high enough, even though he was incapacitated, he could hire a firm to do the work for him, and still make a handsome profit.

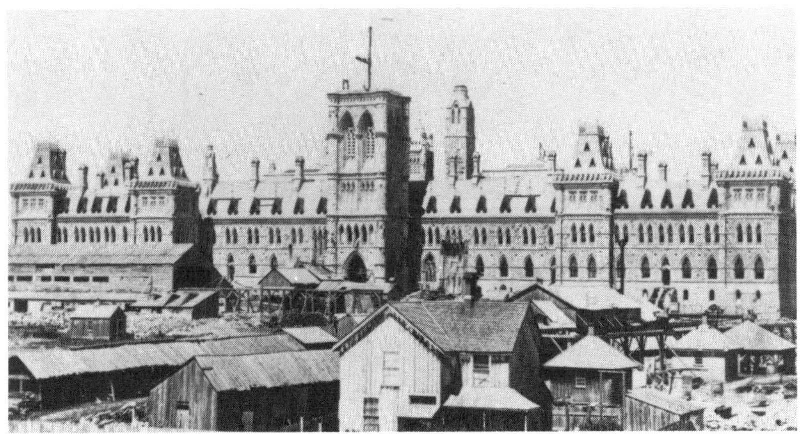

The Parliament Buildings, Ottawa, during the course of construction, 1864.

He wrote to Macdonald once again, and asked for his help. Macdonald replied on 8 July. He assured Benjamin that "You may depend on the nine old Members of the Govt supporting you so far as they can. Indeed I don't see that anyone is particularly interested in opposing you." On the other hand, the contract was to be offered by tender and the other bidders were likely to be the Grand Trunk Railway, the Prescott and Ottawa Railway, and an Ottawa forwarder named Dickinson.[5] There was to be no help from Macdonald, notwithstanding his assurance.[6] It was Macdonald's postscript that delivered the final blow to Benjamin's hopes of a high enough price to make a profit. "I will keep you posted," wrote Macdonald, "make your calculations for a low Bid — & look out for Extras."[7]

By the end of August, still in control of events, Benjamin had completed his property transfers. His lot in Belleville, which he had purchased from Rodney Moore and which was now encumbered by a mortgage, and land he owned in Marmora Township, were transferred to his son Lewis.[8] His 22-room mansion, still subject to mortgages held by George Filliter and Professor George Romanes, mortgages that were 16 and 14 years old, was transferred to his associate and friend Robert Read,[9] under an arrangement that allowed Isabella to continue to live in the house.[10]

Sketch of the Benjamins' house from the "Bird's Eye View of Belleville," 1874.

On 4 September Benjamin gathered his family around him and said his goodbyes.[11] On the following Wednesday morning, 7 September 1864, at ten minutes before two, George Benjamin died.[12] Two days later he was buried in the cemetery of St Thomas' Church in Belleville.[13] He had left no will.[14] He had died, as one of his grandchildren later recalled, "leaving this large family and no money."[15] "I regret to say," his son Mannie wrote his uncle three weeks after Benjamin's death, "his long sickness along with losses sustained through others, and money spent for Elections he had nothing to leave. My brothers and myself with our small incomes will do all we can."[16] "My poor father left his family nothing," he wrote in another letter a month later, "his means were long before his affliction visited him gone[;] his property encumbered and other liabilities incurred upon the assurance that he was to have received the situation that all expected would have been given him."[17]

There was a legacy of bitterness that Benjamin's family felt about his treatment at the hands of the Macdonald. In his letter to his uncle, Mannie referred to Macdonald as "the man who betrayed him."[18] A month later he referred to Macdonald as "the man I look upon as the Murderer of my poor father." "Yes," he continued, "I could fill pages with acts of treachery and base acts committed by Mr. Macdonald against my poor father, but I fear I have already allowed my feelings to carry me quite far enough."[19]

But Benjamin's family survived. Over the next ten years the older sons worked to support the rest of the family. Isabella cut her expenses by moving to a smaller house on the east side of George Street.[20] There was even enough money left over to repay the debts owing on the lot in town and the homestead on Dundas Highway, both of which could now be resold by the family.[21] Isabella's mother, Esther Jacobs, continued to live with her daughter in Belleville until her death on 31 December 1874 at the age of 96.[22] She too was buried in St Thomas' Cemetery.[23]

Isabella Benjamin never remarried. She died in Belleville on 14 October 1903 and was buried in the Anglican cemetery.[24] None of George and Isabella Benjamin's descendants is Jewish. They knew that George had been a Jew who had been baptized just before his death, but a certain pride in his Jewish background had not been extinguished. Lewis Nathan

Esther Jacobs, mother of Isabella Benjamin, photograph, c. 1865.

Isabella Benjamin, photograph, c. 1880.

Benjamin, QC, George and Isabella's second oldest son at the time of George's death, adopted a seal remarkably like the one his father had brought with him when he arrived in Upper Canada in 1834. Over the motto "DEVANT SI JE PUIS," which translates loosely "Ahead, if I can," were two hands, palms facing outwards, with the second and third fingers of each hand spread apart in the manner of the high priest of the Jews during the priestly blessing.[25]

Lewis Nathan Benjamin
adopted a seal remarkably like his father's.

NOTES

[1] George Benjamin to Isaac Buchanan, 18 December 1863, NAC, MG24, D 16, pp. 1644-46.

[2] Information as to the children's jobs appears in *The letters of Sir John A. Macdonald, 1858-1861*, *op. cit.*, p. 258, n. 2 (re. Robert Newberry). *See also* Benjamin to Buchanan, 18 December 1863, *loc. cit.*; E. H. Benjamin to Buchanan, 7 November 1864, *loc. cit.*; E. H. Benjamin to Abraham Cohen, 30 September 1864, *loc. cit.*

[3] St Thomas' Church records, register no. 7-B-4, p. 274.

[4] George Benjamin to Abraham Cohen, 6 May 1864, Abraham Cohen family papers.

[5] Probably Moss Kent Dickinson: *See* Larry Turner, "Moss Kent Dickinson," *Dictionary of Canadian Biography*, vol. XII.

[6] John A. Macdonald to George Benjamin, 8 July 1864, Benjamin family papers.

[7] *Ibid.*

[8] Deed dated and registered 29 August 1864 as nos. B7195 and 225 in the Hastings County Registry Office.

[9] Robert Read (1814-96) was a farmer and butcher in Belleville in the 1840s who was associated with Benjamin as an Orangeman. In 1856 he was appointed county auditor under Benjamin as warden. After Edmund Murney died in August 1861, Read, at Benjamin's urging, ran to fill the vacancy in the Legislative Council. He served on council for Quinte division until 1867 and was conservative MP for Hastings East from 1867 to 1871, when he was appointed to the Senate of Canada. See Dictionary of Canadian Biography, biographical files. Title was transferred to Read by George and Isabella Benjamin by deed dated 29 August 1864 and registered 1 September 1864 as no. E276.

[10] According to the *1864-65 Directory of the County of Hastings* (Belleville, *Intelligencer*, 1865), p. 114, "Mrs. George Benjamin, widow," was still living at her house on the south side of Dundas Street.

[11] Emanuel Hyman Benjamin, Quebec, to Abraham Cohen, Sydney, 30 September 1864, Abraham Cohen family papers. George Benjamin's farewell to his family was recorded by his son.

[12] Emanuel Hyman Benjamin, Belleville, to Abraham Cohen, Sydney, 12 September 1864, Abraham Cohen family papers.

[13] *See* St Thomas' records, register no. 7-B-4, p. 275.

[14] Searches conducted at the PAO.

[15] Probably written by Rosetta Julia Benjamin Gemmell Shaw: "George Benjamin File," Belleville Public Library, Hastings County Historical Society Collection, item no. 2385.

[16] Emanuel Hyman Benjamin to Abraham Cohen, 30 September 1864, Abraham Cohen family papers.

[17] Emanuel Hyam Benjamin to Isaac Buchanan, Hamilton, 7 November 1864, NAC, MG24, D 16, pp. 1623-31.

[18] E. H. Benjamin to Abraham Cohen, 30 September 1864, *loc. cit.*

[19] E. H. Benjamin to Isaac Buchanan, 7 November 1864, *loc. cit.*

[20] The house was the third south from the bridge, *see* "George Benjamin File," *loc. cit.*

[21] On 27 May 1867, by instrument registered as no. F235, Edmund Murney's plan of lot 6, conc. 1, Thurlow Township, was discharged from a mortgage to secure a debt of $200 made by George Benjamin in favour of Uriah West on 16 February 1860 (registered as no. A189, Hastings County Registry Office, Belleville). The title to the house on Dundas Highway (south half of lot 5, conc. 1, Thurlow Township) is somewhat more complicated. On 7 October 1865 Robert Read quit claimed the property to George Romanes, the second mortgage by instrument registered as no. E416. Romanes sold the property to Lewis Nathan Benjamin, George Benjamin's second son, on 9 November 1865, a month later, by deed registered as no. E427. On 17 October 1868 Lewis Benjamin was able to obtain a large mortgage from the Trust and Loan Company (registered as G86).

[22] Louis N. Benjamin to Henrietta Cote, January 1875, Benjamin family papers, Toronto.

[23] Anglican diocesan records, Kingston, register no. 7-B-22, p. 5.

[24] "George C. Benjamin's Family Record," *loc. cit.*

[25] An impression of this seal on red wax on the back of an envelope addressed by Lewis Nathan Benjamin to his fiancée Henrietta Cote on 31 December 1874 is in the possession of descendants of the Benjamin family.

C H A P T E R   X V

Ottawa, 1888

WINTER, 11 JANUARY 1888. SIR JOHN A. MACDONALD SAT AT HIS DESK IN Ottawa, Canada's seat of government. Almost 25 years had passed since Benjamin's death, over 20 since Canada had become a dominion, at confederation. With one interruption, Macdonald had been prime minister for all of that period. The governor general, Lord Lansdowne, had received a note from Colonel Arthur W. Hart of Montreal and, in view of the contents, had sent it over to Macdonald to answer. Hart, a member of the Hart family that had been in Quebec for over a century, expressed a thinly veiled criticism of Macdonald's government, noting that there were no Jews in public office in Canada.[1]

Macdonald's carefully constructed reply started with a defence: "I can only say that I am quite unaware of any prejudice on the parts of the various cabinets that have administered the affairs of the old Province of Canada or of the Dominion against the employment of Jews in the public service." Ever the politician, Macdonald shifted his argument. "The fact is, however, that the Jews as a body have taken perhaps a wiser course in avoiding the worries of political life and have preferred to push their fortune in the various professions and industries open to everybody, in Canada. Of course," he continued, moving now to turn the tables on a perceived opponent, "no person can interfere with the free exercise of the franchise by the electors of this country and they cannot help it if the electors have not hitherto selected any Israelite as their representative." Then the conclusion: "The late George Benjamin of Belleville was a Jew, though I believe he had become a Christian."

Macdonald could be excused for not knowing that Samuel Hart of Nova Scotia, Ezekiel Hart of Lower Canada, Selim Franklin of Vancouver Island, as well as Benjamin were all Israelites when selected by the electors

143

to represent them in their provincial legislatures. So too were Samuel C. Benjamin, Montreal alderman in 1849, William Hyman, mayor of Cap Rosiers in the Gaspé from 1858 to 1882, Lumley Franklin, mayor of Victoria in 1866, and Benjamin, when selected as representatives to municipal office by the electors.

It was harder to understand Macdonald's lack of awareness of Henry Nathan Jr, a Jew who was elected as a supporter of Macdonald's Conservatives in 1873, an Israelite, representing the electors of Victoria, British Columbia.[2]

None of these men were Jewish representatives.[3] They were representatives who were Jewish. They, or their fathers, had come to search out a new land, to escape the restrictions of the old. They were content to live with minimal, organized Jewish communal life, and in some cases with none. They had in common a desire to participate equally in this new land as elected representatives in communities where the vast majority of the population was Christian. They and their families had, to a large extent, assimilated into the culture of the communities they served. They shared a common fate to the extent that almost none of their descendants remain Jewish.

In the end, Benjamin's religion, while perhaps an underlying motivating force in his life, had not been a priority for him, nor had it been an issue for others. He was known to have been a Jew by those who voted for him yet he was elected to public office again and again. He had come to Canada to search out the land. He had ended by putting to rest the question of whether Jews in Canada could be elected to public office and could serve as members of parliament. That was his legacy. Four months before he died he had written to his brother Abraham Cohen in Hebrew. לֹא אִירָא מַה יַּעֲשֶׂה בָּשָׂר לִי — "I will not fear what flesh can do unto me."[4] He had lived up to his ancient family motto.

NOTES

[1] The correspondence is reprinted in part in Sack, *op. cit.*, p. 200. Arthur Wellington Hart (1813-91), eldest son of Benjamin Hart, lived in Toronto from 1834 to 1838.

[2] Henry Nathan Jr was born in London in 1842. He arrived in Victoria with his father in 1862 and set up business as a wholesale merchant. In 1870, at the age of 29, he was elected a member of the Legislative Council of the colony of British Columbia. He was acclaimed as member of the Canadian House of Commons representing Victoria when the province of British Columbia entered confederation on 20 July 1871, and was given the honour as a government supporter of making the address in reply to the speech from the throne at the 1872 session. A director of the Canadian Pacific Railway, he was returned as an MP in the general election of 1873, though Macdonald's Conservatives were defeated over the Pacific Scandal. He retired from public office in 1874 and returned to England in 1880. Leonoff, *op. cit.*, pp. 168-69, and "Pioneer Jewish Merchants," *loc. cit.*, pp. 14-15.

[3] Samuel W. Jacobs, KC, elected to the House of Commons in 1917 for Montreal Saint Lawrence, was the first MP elected as the representative of an area having a significant Jewish population. Large-scale immigration of Jews from Eastern Europe had started in 1882 and expanded after 1896.

[4] George Benjamin to Abraham Cohen, 6 May 1864, *loc. cit.*

George C. Benjamin and Ned Milburn,
two of the Benjamins' grandchildren, c. 1884.

The Benjamin Family Genealogy

ABBREVIATIONS USED

a.k.a.	—	also known as
Aust.	—	Australia
Bell.	—	Belleville
Chic.	—	Chicago
C.W.	—	Canada West
dau.	—	daughter
DSP	—	died without issue
div.	—	divorced
Eng.	—	England
Germ.	—	Germany
La.	—	Louisiana
Mtl.	—	Montreal
New Orl.	—	New Orleans
N.S.W.	—	New South Wales
N.Y.	—	New York
Ott.	—	Ottawa
Penn.	—	Pennsylvania
prob.	—	probably
UNM	—	unmarried

GEORGE BENJAMIN'S FAMILY

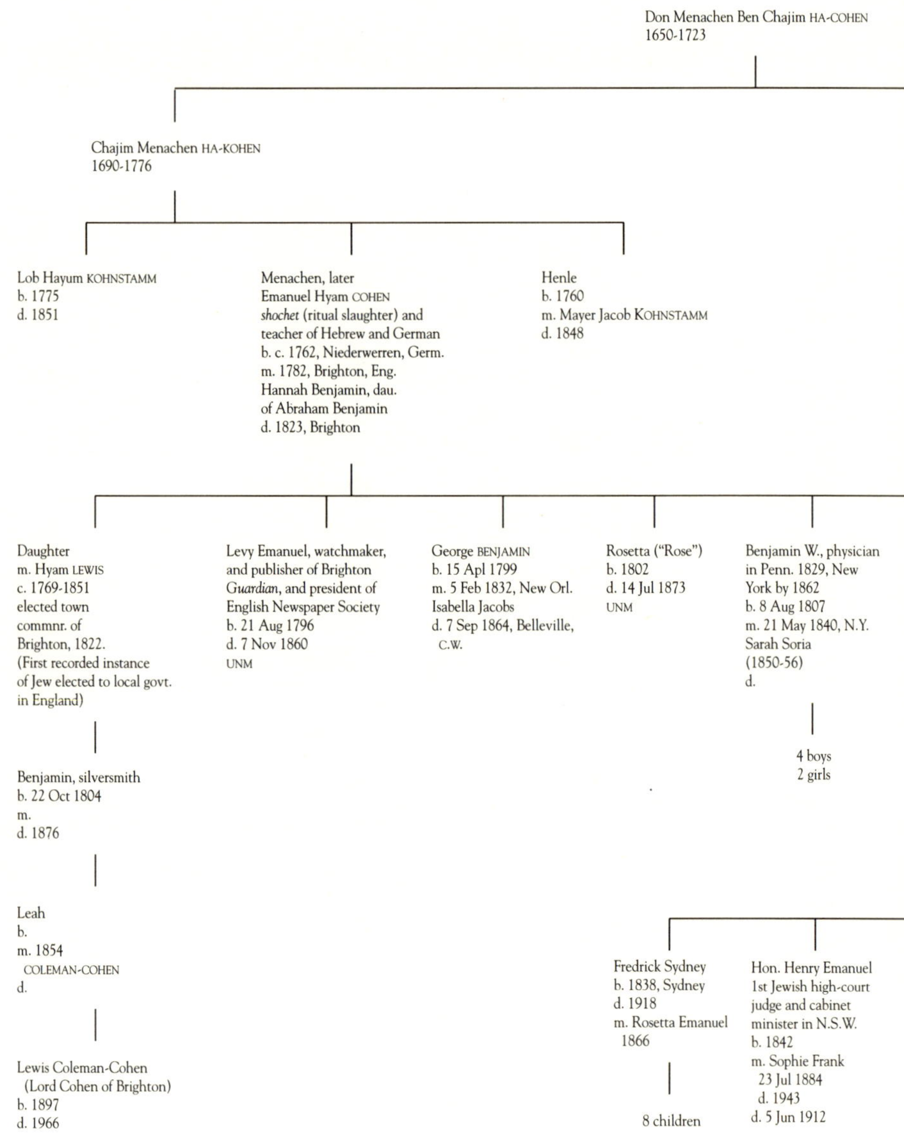

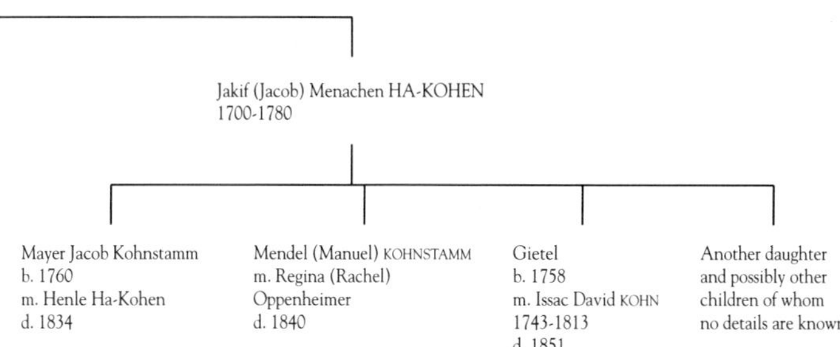

Jakif (Jacob) Menachen HA-KOHEN
1700-1780

Mayer Jacob Kohnstamm
b. 1760
m. Henle Ha-Kohen
d. 1834

Mendel (Manuel) KOHNSTAMM
m. Regina (Rachel)
Oppenheimer
d. 1840

Gietel
b. 1758
m. Issac David KOHN
1743-1813
d. 1851

Another daughter
and possibly other
children of whom
no details are known

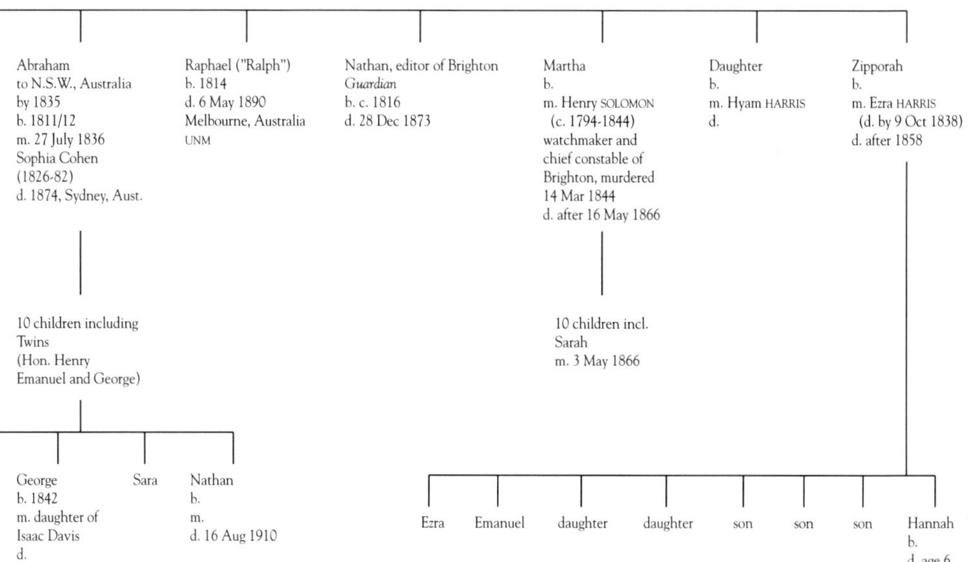

Abraham
to N.S.W., Australia
by 1835
b. 1811/12
m. 27 July 1836
Sophia Cohen
(1826-82)
d. 1874, Sydney, Aust.

Raphael ("Ralph")
b. 1814
d. 6 May 1890
Melbourne, Australia
UNM

Nathan, editor of Brighton
Guardian
b. c. 1816
d. 28 Dec 1873

Martha
b.
m. Henry SOLOMON
 (c. 1794-1844)
watchmaker and
chief constable of
Brighton, murdered
14 Mar 1844
d. after 16 May 1866

Daughter
b.
m. Hyam HARRIS
d.

Zipporah
b.
m. Ezra HARRIS
 (d. by 9 Oct 1838)
d. after 1858

10 children including
Twins
(Hon. Henry
Emanuel and George)

10 children incl.
Sarah
m. 3 May 1866

George
b. 1842
m. daughter of
Isaac Davis
d.

Sara

Nathan
b.
m.
d. 16 Aug 1910

Ezra

Emanuel

daughter

daughter

son

son

son

Hannah
b.
d. age 6
by 1838

GEORGE AND ISABELLA BENJAMIN
AND SOME OF THEIR DESCENDANTS

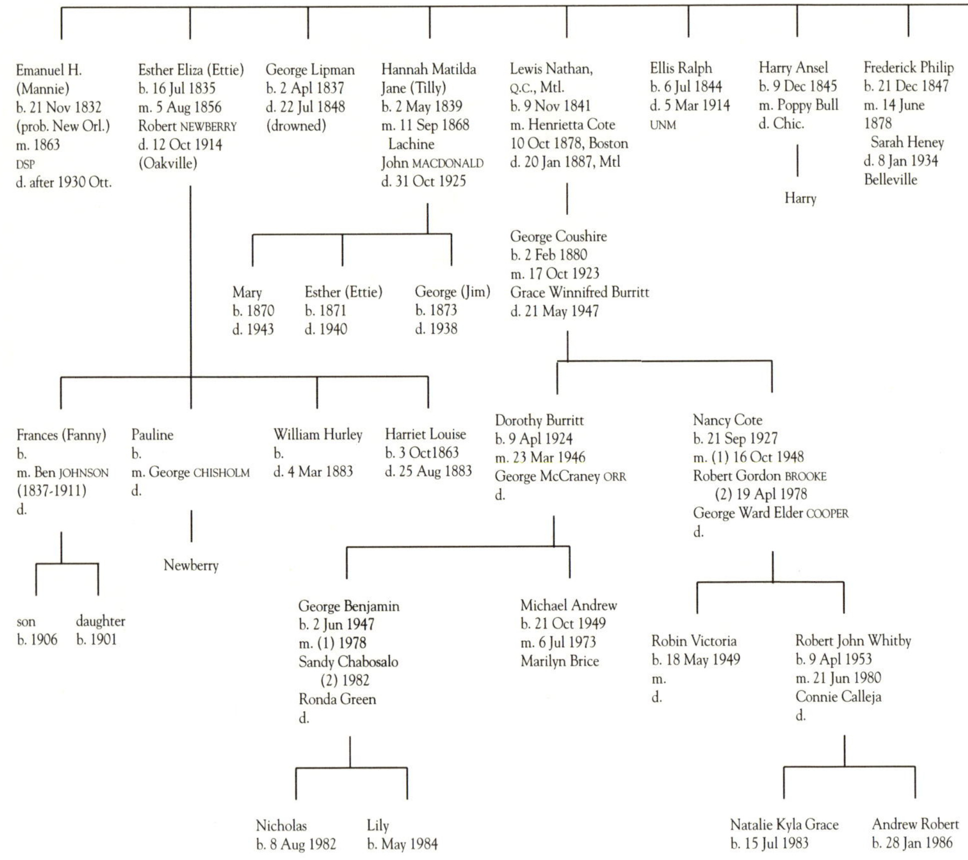

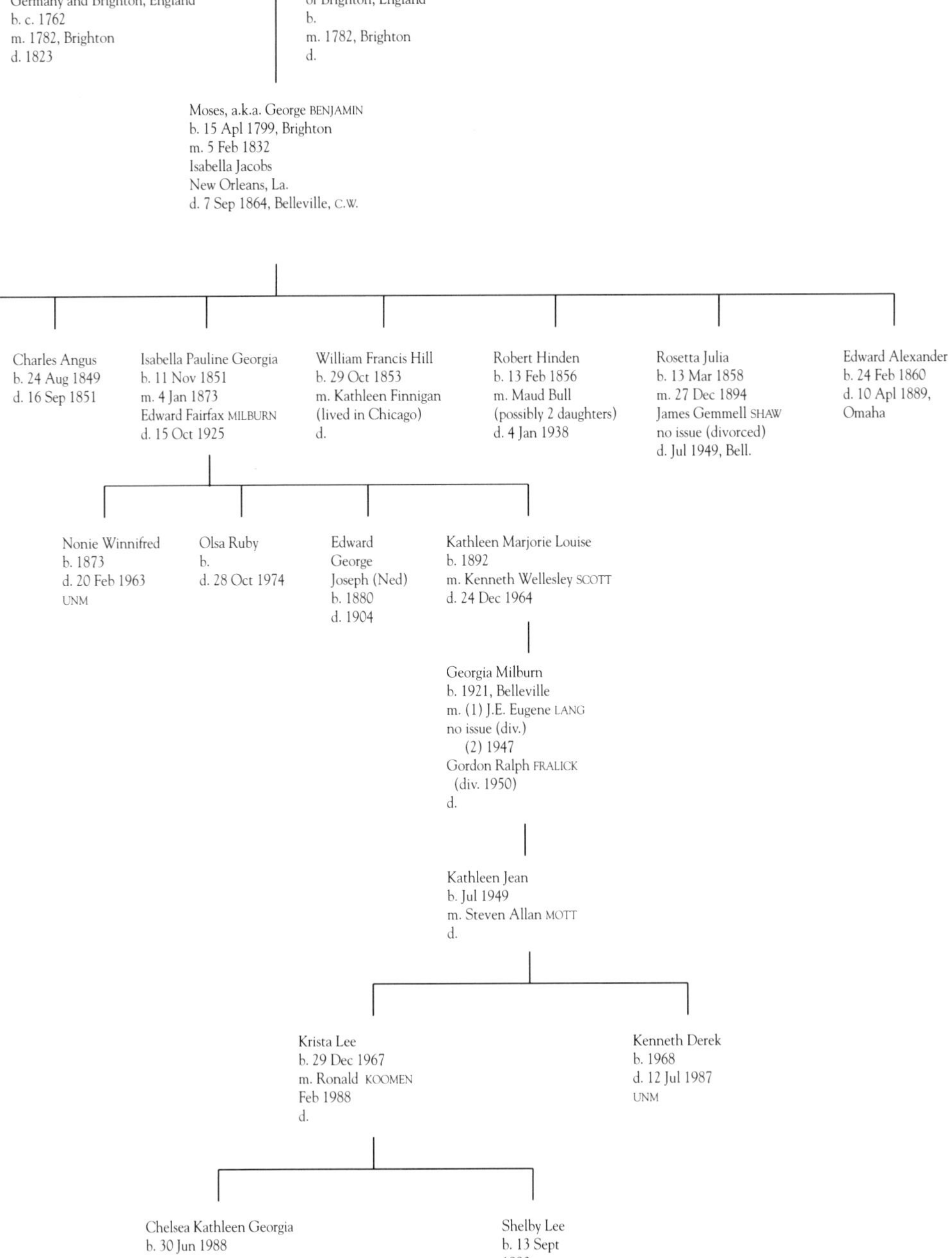

Emanual Hyam COHEN of Niederwerren, Germany and Brighton, England
b. c. 1762
m. 1782, Brighton
d. 1823

Hannah, daughter of Abraham Benjamin of Brighton, England
b.
m. 1782, Brighton
d.

Moses, a.k.a. George BENJAMIN
b. 15 Apl 1799, Brighton
m. 5 Feb 1832
Isabella Jacobs
New Orleans, La.
d. 7 Sep 1864, Belleville, C.W.

Charles Angus
b. 24 Aug 1849
d. 16 Sep 1851

Isabella Pauline Georgia
b. 11 Nov 1851
m. 4 Jan 1873
Edward Fairfax MILBURN
d. 15 Oct 1925

William Francis Hill
b. 29 Oct 1853
m. Kathleen Finnigan
(lived in Chicago)
d.

Robert Hinden
b. 13 Feb 1856
m. Maud Bull
(possibly 2 daughters)
d. 4 Jan 1938

Rosetta Julia
b. 13 Mar 1858
m. 27 Dec 1894
James Gemmell SHAW
no issue (divorced)
d. Jul 1949, Bell.

Edward Alexander
b. 24 Feb 1860
d. 10 Apl 1889, Omaha

Nonie Winnifred
b. 1873
d. 20 Feb 1963
UNM

Olsa Ruby
b.
d. 28 Oct 1974

Edward George Joseph (Ned)
b. 1880
d. 1904

Kathleen Marjorie Louise
b. 1892
m. Kenneth Wellesley SCOTT
d. 24 Dec 1964

Georgia Milburn
b. 1921, Belleville
m. (1) J.E. Eugene LANG
no issue (div.)
(2) 1947
Gordon Ralph FRALICK
(div. 1950)
d.

Kathleen Jean
b. Jul 1949
m. Steven Allan MOTT
d.

Krista Lee
b. 29 Dec 1967
m. Ronald KOOMEN
Feb 1988
d.

Kenneth Derek
b. 1968
d. 12 Jul 1987
UNM

Chelsea Kathleen Georgia
b. 30 Jun 1988

Shelby Lee
b. 13 Sept 1990

ISABELLA BENJAMIN'S FAMILY

Lipman JACOBS
b. Netherlands
d. New Orleans
m. 1792 Esther (*née* Abraham [?])
(b. 17 December 1778, d. 31 December 1874, Belleville)

Isabella
b. 8 March 1819, New Orleans
m. George BENJAMIN
(5 February 1832, New Orleans)
d. 14 October 1903, Belleville

Jacques ("Jaques") or Jacob
b.
m.
d. Amsterdam

CHART I SOURCE NOTES

1. David Spector, "The Jews of Brighton, 1770-1900," *Jewish Historical Society of England Transactions*, XXII (1970), pp. 42-52, and "Brighton Jewry Reconsidered," *ibid.*, XXX (1987-88), pp. 91-124.

2. C. Theodore Marx, "Kohnstamm/Cohen Family Genealogy," mss, Wembly Park, Middlesex, England.

3. David J. Benjamin, "Henry Emanuel Cohen," *Australian Jewish Historical Society Journal*, II (1948), pp. 524-61.

4. The birthdate of Benjamin Solomons appears in the records of the Great Synagogue, London, as cited by Cecil Roth, *The rise of provincial Jewry* (London, Jewish Monthly, 1950), p. 39.

5. Abraham Cohen family papers and letterbooks in the possession of Henry Robert Cohen, Mossman, N. S. W.

6. Spector and Marx are of the opinion that Hyam Lewis was a brother-in-law to the children of Emanuel Hyam and Hannah Cohen, having married one of their daughters born before Levy Emanuel Cohen. According to David Spector, in 1827 Levy Emanuel Cohen was summoned before Sir David Scott, a local magistrate of Brighton, to answer the charge that he had refused to serve as a "special constable." Cohen pleaded that he was "a minister of religion." When Sir David suggested that he might want to call his "brother-in-law, Hyam Lewis," as a witness, Cohen declined as they were not on speaking terms. On the other hand, see Levy Emanuel Cohen to Abraham Cohen, 29 July 1850: "Your uncle, Hyam Lewis, is in a very precarious state; his sand is nearly run out, he is upwards of 80." Both Levy Emanuel Cohen and Abraham Cohen were brothers of George Benjamin: Abraham Cohen family papers.

7. Henry Robert Cohen, "Summary of the Abraham Cohen Family in Australia," mss, Australian Jewish Historical Society, Great Synagogue, Sydney, N. S. W.

8. Donald Cohen, "Genealogy of the descendants of Frederick Sydney Cohen and Rosetta Emanuel," mss, Australian Jewish Historical Society, Great Synagogue, Sydney, N. S. W.

9. Benjamin W. Cohen signed a "Declaration" of his intention to become a citizen of the United States of America at Philadelphia, 5 June 1833. A copy is in the possession of C. T. Marx; the original is in the Philadelphia City Archives, unknown volume, p. 289.

10. Levy Emanuel Cohen's obituary was published in the Brighton *Guardian*, 21 and 28 November 1860, reprinted in the *London Jewish Chronicle*, November 1860, pp. 2-41.

CHART II SOURCE NOTES

1. *Intelligencer*, Belleville (mfm at Archives of Ontario) as to the following marriages: Esther Benjamin to Robert Newberry (8 August 1856), Matilda Benjamin to John Macdonald (18 September 1868), Isabella Benjamin to Edward F. Milburn (5/6 June 1873), Lewis Nathan Benjamin to Henrietta Cote (16 October 1878), and Frederick P. Benjamin to Sarah Heney (14 June 1878).

2. Archives of the Anglican Archdiocese, as to baptisms of the Benjamin children: register no. 7-B-3, pp. 253, 293, 320, 360, 418; as to the death and burial of Charles Angus Benjamin, register no. 7-B-3, p. 409; as to the baptisms of George and Isabella Benjamin, register no. 7-B-4, p. 274; as to the death and burial of George Benjamin, register no. 7-B-4, p. 275.

3. Henrietta Cote, "George C. Benjamin's Family Record, 1914," in the possession of the Benjamin family, Toronto.

4. Headstones at the cemetery, St Thomas' Church, Belleville.

5. "Notes on the Benjamin Family," Hastings County Historical Society Collection, item no. 2385, Belleville Public Library.

6. As to death of Isabella Jacobs, 14 October 1903, *see* St Thomas' Church burials, 1872-1979, no. 345.5, Belleville Public Library.

7. See George Benjamin's Hebrew prayer-book as to marriage of George and Isabella Benjamin and births of Emanuel Hyman, Esther Eliza, George Lipman, Hannah Matilda, Lewis Nathan, Ellis Ralph, Harry Ansel, and Frederick Philip.

8. [Mackenzie Bowell], "George Benjamin, Esq.," *Intelligencer*, 9 September 1864.

CHART III SOURCE NOTES

1. According to "George C. Benjamin's Family Record, 1914," by Henrietta Cote Benjamin, widow of Louis Nathan Benjamin, in the possession of the Benjamin family, Isabella Benjamin was born in New Orleans in 1819. Her mother was Esther Abraham, born 17 Dec. 1778, married Lipman Jacobs 1792, died in Belleville, Ont., 31 Dec. 1874.

2. George Benjamin's Hebrew prayer-book states: "Married 5 February 1832/George Benjamin to Isabella Jacobs." According to "George C. Benjamin's Family Record, 1914," George and Isabella Benjamin were married on that date in New Orleans.

3. According to the records at the Archives of the Anglican Archdiocese, Kingston, Ont., register no. 7-B-22, p. 5, Esther Jacobs, widow of Lipman Jacobs, died 31 December 1874, aged 96, and was buried in the cemetery of St Thomas' Church

in Belleville on 3 January 1875. The 1874 date of death is confirmed by a letter from Lewis Nathan Benjamin in Montreal to his *fiancée* Henrietta Cote, 31 December 1874, where he states, "I have just received a telegram from Belleville saying that My Grand-Mother died at three o'clock this morning ... ," Benjamin family papers. A further search of the archdiocesan registers does not document a baptism for Esther Jacobs.

4. There is differing evidence regarding Esther Jacobs' maiden name. According to Rosetta Gemmell Shaw, daughter of George and Isabella Benjamin, "My grand-mother on Mother's side was a Heine." Benjamin family papers, Hastings County Historical Society Collection, item no. 2385, Belleville Pubic Library. The brothers Armand and Michel Heine, cousins of the German Jewish poet Heinrich Heine, settled in New Orleans in 1842: Bertram W. Korn, *Early Jews of New Orleans* (Waltham, Mass., American Jewish Historical Society, 1969), pp. 123-24. Rosetta Gemmell Shaw's note gives additional information: "When her husband died, she came to mother's to live." This indicates that Esther Jacobs had come to live with her daughter Isabella Benjamin. The note also refers to "Jaques," apparently the only brother of Isabella, who came to Belleville to visit but subsequently returned to Amsterdam, where he had been born.

5. Isabella Benjamin died in Belleville on 14 October 1903: St Thomas' Church burials, 1872-1979, no. 345.5, Belleville Public Library.

6. Further research in New Orleans has not located the family of Lipman Jacobs in that city in the relevant period. A "Lewis Lipman Jacobs of the City of Mobile" executed a conveyance to Hypolyte Robelin of New Orleans, recorded by W. Y. Lewis, notary public, on 23 February 1843: City of New Orleans Conveyance Office, Parish of New Orleans, book 35, p. 8. Searches in Mobile, Alabama, have not confirmed the residence of a person by that name during the relevant period. According to census records, there was only one "L. Jacobs" family in New Orleans during the 1930s: United States Census, 1830, mfm M19, roll no. 45, p. 235. "L. Jacobs" also appears in the census for 1820. In the 1840 census "L. Jacobs" appears in Municipality Number 3, 2nd District (mfm M704, roll no. 134, p. 147) as well as in Jno. P. Walden's Division, Parish of New Orleans (mfm M704, roll no. 133, p. 23). There are no similar entries in the 1810 or 1850 censuses. The "L. Jacobs" in New Orleans was Levy Jacobs rather than Lipman Jacobs. Levy Jacobs had come to New Orleans from Holland before 1820. He had a wife named Esther (*née* Cohen) and a daughter named Isabella, and died on 8 May 1843: Records of deaths and burials of the Gates of Mercy (Shaarei Chesed Congregation), Rare Book and Manuscript Room, Tulane University, item 224. Levy Jacobs had at least five children, including an older son, Levy Jr, born in the Netherlands about 1797. The estate of Levy Jacobs Jr (d. 2 June 1855) is recorded as entry no. 9102 in the Second District Court, Parish of New Orleans (mfm) at the New Orleans Public Library.

PICTURE CREDITS

COVER

George Benjamin, oil painting by William Sawyer, c. 1859
Hastings County Museum/Hastings County Historical Society,
Ref. P 748 Neg. 178, HC 1477

CHAPTER I

Page 2   Private
Page 3   Private
Page 4   Private

CHAPTER II

Page 9   David Spector and the Brighton Reference Library Archives
Page 11   David Spector and the Brighton Reference Library Archives
Page 12   Dennis Rose, *Life times and recorded works of Richard Dighton
            (1752-1814) actor, artist and printseller and thence of his artist sons*
            (Lewes, 1981), p. 44
            David Spector
Page 14   David Spector and the Brighton Reference Library Archives
Page 15   *Patriot and Farmer's Monitor* (Toronto), 18 July 1834, p. 3
            Archives of Ontario
Page 17   Archives of Ontario, Burrowes' Sketches C-1 No. 110
Page 19   Private

CHAPTER III

Page 24   *Intelligencer*, 11 Oct. 1834
            Hastings County Historical Society
Page 26   *British Whig* (Kingston), 27 April 1837
Page 27   *Whig Standard*, Kingston
Page 28   *Intelligencer*, 11 Oct. 1834
            Hastings County Historical Society, Ref. No. HC4357
Page 30   *Intelligencer*, 11 Oct. 1834
            Advert., Ref. No. HC4360

CHAPTER V

Page 46   H. J. Morgan, *Types of Canadian women* (Toronto, 1903), p. 238
            National Archives of Canada, Ref. No. C7043
Page 47   *Literary Garland*, vol. 1, no. 11 (November 1843)
            University of Toronto, Thomas Fisher Rare Book Library

INDEX

Married February 1832
Geory Benjamin to Isabella Jacobs.
————

Born 21st Nov 1832.
Emanuel Hyman son of George
& Isabella Benjamin.
                              G Benjamin
                ————

Born 16th July 1835.
    Esther Eliza daughter of George
and Isabella Benjamin
                              G Benjamin
                ————

Born 2d April 1837
    George Lipman, son of
George & Isabella Benjamin
                              G W Benjamin

Born 2 May 1839
Hannah Michtil a daughter
of George & Isabella Benjamin